SUNNY SIDE UP

SUNNY SIDE UP

by

Arthur Marshall

HAMISH HAMILTON · LONDON

HAMISH HAMILTON LTD

Penguin Books Ltd, 27 Wrights Lane, London W8 5TZ (Publishing & Editorial)
and Harmondsworth, Middlesex, England (Distribution & Warehouse)
Viking Penguin Inc., 40 West 23rd Street, New York, New York 10010, U.S.A.
Penguin Books Australia Ltd, Ringwood, Victoria, Australia
Penguin Books Canada Limited, 2801 John Street, Markham, Ontario, Canada L3R 1B4
Penguin Books (N.Z.) Ltd, 182–190 Wairau Road, Auckland 10, New Zealand

First published in Great Britain 1987 by
Hamish Hamilton Ltd

British Library Cataloguing in Publication Data
Marshall, Arthur, *1910–*
Sunny side up.
I. Title
828' .91407   PR 6063. A76
ISBN 0-241-12358-5

Printed and bound in Great Britain by
Butler & Tanner, Frome and London

CONTENTS

FOREWORD

Those readers whom in the past I have been fortunate enough to meet upon the printed page will know better than to expect from me anything in the way of profundity. Profundity is often productive of Thoughts or, to describe them more impressively, *Pensées* and almost all *Pensées* are depressing. They concern Life and its livers and they invariably communicate gloom. Thoreau's famous 'The mass of men lead lives of quiet desperation' is a case in point, doubtfully veracious though the statement may be. I have written elsewhere about what must have been the sad disadvantage of being a member of the La Rochefoucauld family, forced to receive, like stinging blows in the face, fifteen sour *Pensées* a day, all of them of a lowering nature and concerning the alleged selfishness and vanity and egotism and the generally unsatisfactory behaviour of the human race. If La Rochefoucauld ever saw a French boy scout helping an old lady across the *rue*, he forgot to mention it.

What is the opposite of profundity? Frivolity or levity perhaps? Whatever it is, it is what you will find here. I was born frivolous and frivolous I have remained. I in no way regret it. I may have skated lightly across the surface of life but I have, and lucky I have been, skated happily. As to my frivolity, 'two examples will suffice', as the exam papers used to say before going on to request you to 'state your reasons and draw a map.'

It was in my second term as a Cambridge undergraduate in 1929 and I was having tea with my friend, Maurice Johnson, in the Sidney Street Fuller's, famous for its walnut and cream layer sponges and one of a chain of admirable tea and cake shops that were in those carefree days such an amenity in English towns. We had both discovered, and mercifully early on in our Cambridge careers, the importance of not attending lectures, finding them to be a waste of valuable time and muddling to the mind. I forget now the earlier events of that particular day but I

1

expect they had been leisurely – a protracted, dressing-gowned breakfast in my rooms, a glance at the *Morning Post*, a stroll to the Amateur Dramatic Club to rehearse a musical item for the forthcoming Smoking Concert ('Can Geoffrey please give me a few mounting chords to get me to centre stage?'), lunch somewhere, a cinema (Clara Bow looking roguish) and thence to Fuller's and Maurice.

As we sat there munching and probably discussing the charms of Miss Gertrude Lawrence or, if not her, Miss Beatrice Lillie, we suddenly heard somebody, keen for nourishment, addressing a question to the waitress, and an unusual one in a Fuller's which didn't really go in for cooked dishes. The question was 'Have you scrambled eggs, by any chance?' but the words came out, in a sort of anxious falsetto, as 'Hev you scrembled eggs, by any chornce?' Enraptured, we looked eagerly up at the questioner and saw a tall, thin, rather wispy young man with rabbity teeth and lank fair hair. He had no monocle but gave the impression of wearing one. Had he applied for membership of Wodehouse's Drones Club he would have been immediately accepted. In riper years he could have understudied that superb farce actor, Ralph Lynn. Physically he was the double of every 'silly ass' role then popular in films and on the stage but it was the voice and the plaintive request for eggs and the 'by any chance' that got us.

By means of outstanding detective work Maurice discovered that the egg-fancier was in Trinity, was reading geography, was in his third year, lived in what sounded like a stately home and possessed one of those upper-crust names that rely rather heavily on the letter 'y', as it might be Wylyss-Wylte. For the next term and a half we made it our business to dog his footsteps in order to hear him, just once more, ask for scrambled eggs. My landlord had a telephone and kindly took messages and on Maurice flashing me the news that Wylyss-Wylte had been seen making for the quaintly named Scotch Hoose Café in the Market Place, I would be on to my bike in a trice. We tracked him down and pursued him all over Cambridge. As time went on he came to wear a slightly perplexed and persecuted look, knowing full well that as soon as he sat down for tea in a place of refreshment he would almost certainly find Maurice or me alongside and expectantly hovering.

All in vain, alas. If Wylyss-Wylte ever again wanted scrambled eggs at tea-time, he managed to fight down the gluttonous urge. We watched him eat buns galore, endless marzipan slices and yard upon yard of hot buttered toast, but never again did he ask for eggs. However, I did have one small success. I managed to bump into him, accidentally on purpose, don't you know, in Trinity Street, and my vigorous apologies were cut short with a remark that also relied on the letter 'y' — 'Quayte may fault, Ay do assure you'. And then he went down and our chornce was gone. Incidentally, the words 'went down' describe all too accurately the descent from what was then for many of us an idle, pleasurable, privileged and often frivolous life into its harsher realities.

And thus it has gone on. In the days when hand-delivered telegrams existed and were relatively cheap and widely used, I was wishful to thank a fairly mature woman friend for an extreme kindness that she had done me, at considerable cost to herself. Deciding that this merited a Greetings Telegram, I went to the nearest London Post Office and drafted a message which began with the light-hearted phrase MY GOODNESS WHAT A TRUMP YOU ARE but which reached its destination as MY GOODNESS WHAT A FRUMP YOU ARE. This has given me, and to a rather lesser extent my friend, enormous pleasure for a good many years. Such is the pattern.

There follow offerings that, with very few exceptions, have not before had the distinction of finding themselves between hard covers — a selection, entitled Sunday Best, of my fortnightly *Sunday Telegraph* pieces, some of my weekly articles from the *New Statesman*, a 'literary' discursion or two, and a random choice of the extraordinary number of surprising facts that a reviewer of biographical books gathers as he plods his often weary way. I am grateful to the editors for their permissions to print.

Oh and by the way, some readers may consider that I refer rather too often to Mrs Thatcher and Lady Macbeth. For those unacquainted with the ladies, the former was our Prime

Minister at the time of writing and the latter was a noted regicide who possessed the very unusual skill of being able to sleep, walk and talk all at the same time, an ability that has been sadly overlooked by the numerous assessors of her character and achievements.

SUNDAY BEST

IN HALL IF WET

As most country and village dwellers will know, we are now slap-bang in the middle of the church fête season (proceeds to repairs to the poor old roof which, for the umpteenth time, is being rescued from change and decay). Last Saturday the fête was at Little Bedding. Next Saturday it will be the turn of Great Bedding (twinned with Merde-la-Profiterole).

Everywhere vicarage gardens have been resplendent with bunting, the local Morris Dancers have clattered themselves to a standstill, and near a side door into the house a lop-sided notice has brought its very own message of comfort and cheer, displaying a warm regard for things temporal ('TOILETS'). Laden stalls have graced the lawn, there have been competitions for the kiddies ('*Isn't* that Dawn Medlicott a little madam!') and the Hoop-La trestle has collapsed into the Nearly New display.

Let me instantly confess that I am a very old hand at garden fêtes. For many years my mother was President of our Women's Institute and there is little I do not know about fêtes, bazaars, Social Half Hours, home-made cake and Talks invitingly called How To Make a Comfy Pouffe Out of Next to Nothing.

On one occasion the fête was in our own Berkshire garden, in the days when I was young and given to pranks (about 12 I suppose). The weather was hot and summery, the flower borders were at their best, everything was in readiness and, wishful to brighten the proceedings, I constructed a large notice-board and wrote upon it DON'T GET STUNG BY THE BEES. COME TO THE STALLS INSTEAD. But my mother feared it might discourage trade and my merry joke was banned.

In those days all fêtes were opened by a lady of title. The relatively modest title of Hon was the most popular. The supply of Hons seemed inexhaustible (perhaps they could be

7

ordered from Harrods). They just materialised for the afternoon and were never heard of again. They appeared merely to exist to open fêtes. They were always married to gentlemen with three initials and were called The Hon Mrs J. C. B. Paynte or The Hon Mrs F. L. H. Crumppe.

The Hon Mrs Crumppe always arrived in a vast, chauffeur-driven Daimler ('I've told Jenner to return in forty minutes'),

The Hon. Mrs Crumppe always arrived in a vast,
chauffeur-driven Daimler

was attired in voluminous flowered material and, though seeming never to know quite where she was, graciously unbent to order. Perhaps Harrods also supplied the Hons with scripts, for the words were unchanging: 'It gives me considerable pleasure to throw open your little fête'. The adjective 'little' kept us all in our place and for the word 'fête' Mrs Crumppe provided a French accent, bringing with it a hint of Deauville and a chic world plainly denied to the rest of us.

She then toured the stalls ('Clever fingers!'), made a few simple purchases ('I must get something for my husband. What have you that is edible and kind to teeth?') and then ('Ah, there's Jenner! I mustn't keep him waiting') smartly left.

Sometimes one of the money-making features of a fête is, towards the end of the afternoon, the Lucky Draw for an assortment of generously donated prizes — anything from a Decorated Fruit Basket to a smallish bottle of ketchup. Numbered tickets have previously been sold and the ticket counterfoils have been placed in a large container and the vicar's wife, playfully stirring ('I promise not to peep!'), draws out the first winning counterfoil.

The things to realise here are that (a) the prize winner has invariably long since left the fête, and (b) the name on the counterfoil is quite illegible. This doesn't, however, prevent an attempt to locate the winner. Mrs Vicar dons her specs. 'Ticket number 481 . . . I can't *quite* read the name . . . I think it's . . . I think it's a Miss, or Mrs, Ointment. Would you announce it, dear?' The Vicar then lets fly down his megaphone. 'Will Miss, or Mrs, Ointment please come forward to receive her prize. Miss Ointment, we have something for you. Miss or Mrs, Ointment?'

No response and so they try again. 'Oh dear, it's all too difficult. Ticket number 173. I *think* this is a Mrs Coddlebum.' 'Will Mrs Coddlebum please come forward to receive her prize. Mrs Coddlebum, we have something for you. Mrs Coddlebum?'

If *your* name chances to be either Ointment or Coddlebum, a poker-work motto (DON'T WORRY. IT WON'T HAPPEN) and a set (one missing) of kebab skewers await you.

Z-Z-Z-Z-Z

My grip on most foreign languages is very far from secure and for many years now I have understood, from information passed to me by somebody whom I now suspect of pulling my *gamba* (or leg), that the Italian word for Hong Kong is Honka Konka and that similarly 'ping pong' comes out in the mellifluous tongue of Dante as 'pinka ponka'.

And therefore, if an Italian friend were to invite you to join him in our far-off colony for a game of table tennis, a social excitement that might happen to anybody, you would be playing pinka ponka in Honka Konka. I just mention it.

But having recently returned from an agreeable holiday in Italy, for which trip I was at pains to brush up my Italiano in order to be able to give as good as I got in the way of *'bon giorno'* and 'kindly pass the spaghetti', I am now in a position to be of help, by courtesy of the Italian language, to fellow writers.

As all producers of fiction will know, the question of the choice of names for their imaginary characters is a vital one. Say, for example, that Thomas Hardy, writing *Tess of the D'Urbervilles*, had decided instead to call the heroine 'Maud of the D'Urbervilles', it wouldn't have been the same thing at all. What if Shakespeare had named his young lovers 'Romeo and Monica'? Well then, how does 'Gertrude by Gaslight' grab you? Hopeless, all of them. The best authors hit, as we see, the nominal nail firmly on the head and it is to them that I offer, searching as they may be for what to call some smouldering southern beauty, an Italian name, the arresting one of 'Zanzara'.

Almost any word with a 'z' in it is of interest — one has merely to think of ozone, marzipan, zeppelins and Daz — and Zanzara has, as you see, two of them. It is a richly promising name that would not be out of place in the works of Ouida or Elinor Glyn or Anthony Hope (after all, *The Prisoner of Zenda* has got a 'z' in it too).

I see her as the notorious and beautiful Countess Zanzara who drives men wild all over the Balkans. In younger days she spent her time creating havoc on the Orient Express at a period when the train was given over to intrigue and adventuresses rather than to murder. Wherever she goes, her famous emeralds are to be seen on her heaving bosom, doomed jewels with a curse on them and heaving, with the bosom, now up, now down.

The Count, her husband, has long since died of a broken heart, for she is pitiless, a heartless devil. 'There goes La Zanzara' envious women used to hiss to each other in the '30s as she swayed by, smiling mockingly, dressed from head to foot in chinchilla and on her way to reserve a sleeper on the Blue Train (you never know, some Michael Arlen character might still be wandering about the continent).

I myself last saw the Countess Zanzara about two weeks ago and in my Italian hotel bedroom. She had entered under cover of darkness and was hovering, a thing of spite and venom, about three feet above my head. I did what any of us would have done. I shot her mercilessly down with a squirt from my anti-zanzara chemical spray. Only you and I need to know that *Zanzara* means 'mosquito'. As a name for an enchantress it would fool readers of romantic fiction all along the line.

The Italian language really abounds in name possibilities, many of which may have delighted our own ace name-provider, Charles Dickens. How eagerly he would have pounced on Miss Trambusto, quaint old Mrs Tuta (say it TOOT-ER) and a fiery opera singer called 'La Stuzzicadenti'. The fact that the three words mean 'fuss', 'mechanic's overall' and 'toothpick' need worry nobody.

And finally there is Signor Francobollo, a name so round and open and jolly and reminiscent of the Cheeryble Brothers themselves. But it means, alas, a postage-stamp, an object which, so outrageous are our postal charges, can only be spoken of in displeased whispers.

CHIL-DREN'S COR-NER

A member of the Assistant Masters and Mistresses Association has complained that newspapers cater insufficiently for young readers, implying that a part of every paper should always be devoted to interesting the minds of children and bringing them enjoyment and profit. Before such criticism can possibly be levelled at the *Sunday Telegraph*, a newspaper ever first in the field, we are happy to print suitable children's magazine sections for kiddies of varying ages, from tots to teenagers, a feature which may, or may not, be continued in future editions.

The Editor's Letter

Hel-lo Chil-dren,

First, a word about the great big world. You may have heard grown-ups talking about a place called Russia (you say it RUSH-ER). Well, Russia has got some lands that do not be-long to it, and this is not nice. In fact, it is nas-ty. Great Bri-tain used to have such lands too, but they were called Co-lo-nies and an em-pire, and that is nice and not nas-ty at all.

If you went down to a town (see, we have made a lit-tle rhyme!) called Do-ver and looked a-cross the sea and if it wasn't rain-ing for once, you would see a place called France. It is full of peo-ple who eat frogs' legs, which is not very nice for frogs. In fact, it al-so is nas-ty.

Why not see if you can draw a frog? There will be pri-zes for the best sent in. Or would you like to 'have a go' at jol-ly old Mr Toad? Did you know that the French word for toad is *crapaud* (say him CRAP-OH)! There now! We have learnt a French word!

Next week I shall tell you all a-bout Bri-tish Ley-land. It sounds like a co-lo-ny, don't you think? See if you can guess what they do there (there is a cle-ver say-ing which goes 'Your guess is as good as mine').

Good-bye, chil-dren.
Love from Uncle Arthur

For a really wet afternoon
We suggest that you pull out the attractive 'pull-out' of our leader, Mrs Thatcher, cut round her dotted line (careful with that lovely hair-do!) and then get out your paints and colour her. Remember that many people consider that the prettiest colour of all is blue. I expect that some of you will want to mount her on cardboard and then prop her up on your Trophy Shelf! She seems to be smiling right at you, does she not? Why not write a short imaginary conversation between her and Husband Denis over brunch at No. 10? Send it in and perhaps win a prize. First prize: a day at the Public Record Office. Second prize: two days at the Public Record Office.

Puzzle Corner
See if you can spot the 'odd-man-out' in each of the following:

(1) Apples, oranges, bananas, fish fingers, pears.
(2) Boadicea, Grace Darling, Flora Macdonald, Mr Heath, Florence Nightingale.
(3) 21, 81, 71, 492, 31.

Answers next Sunday and you've really got heaps of time to puzzle them all out, so get cracking, Einsteins!

Poetry Competition
Write a modern version of 'Monday's child is fair of face' making the kiddies just as naughty as ever you can and we suggest that you begin with 'Monday's child has pulled a face' or 'Monday's child is quite a case'. Book prizes for the naughtiest. If you can't get quite all the naughtinesses into one poem, then send in two or three. The editor will be delighted. (You bet! *Ed*.)

Answers to Correspondents

Puzzled, Cleckheaton   Though some folk seem to think that excessive hair means virility, Mr Healey's eyebrows are not a sign of anything special, as far as we can tell. Your letter was well written but note that there is no 'e' in 'bushy'.

Worried, Bude   We see nothing wrong in your aunty purchasing bottles of Cyprus sherry 'by the crateful' and you should not be so quick to criticise an adult. Alcohol can be a valuable stimulant and maybe she is involved in some taxing professional work. The time to worry will be when your aunty starts to tumble over rather a lot.

MORE NEXT WEEK

THEY ALSO SERVE

The optimists among us who, face to face with what may be rather a trying new year, look keenly about us for hopeful signs of improvement, economic or otherwise, will have been greatly cheered by the announcement that a School for British Butlers has opened in Dulwich.

It is situated at a residence called Belair Mansion, the very name of which has about it a solid and reassuring Victorian ring. This can surely only mean that a new wave of prosperity will shortly be ours. Backward countries don't have butlers, do they? Well there you are then!

We all know, from books and the theatre if not from life, what butlers are expected to do. They glide hither and thither. They make impressive appearances at front doors. They enter dining-rooms with decanters of intoxicants. They cough discreetly and are of portly build. They raise their eyebrows quite a lot in disapproval, and on seaside piers and in peep-shows, they see things sometimes denied to the rest of us.

In the present climate of social change and if all else fails, how would one oneself make out as a butler after, naturally, the Belair Advanced Course? The slightly pop-eyed look and the double chins are with me already. The slow and dignified, politer words than 'sluggish', progress from place to place presents no difficulty. The white hair and the portly build are there for the asking. The decanter might be less full than expected when I bring it in but after all, in a large household, who's counting?

I shall call myself either 'Treadgold' or 'Merryweather' for any intending butler must take great care to bear a suitable surname and 'Marshall' would get you nowhere. Nobody has ever bettered Wodehouse's butlers' names of Beech and Keggs though reality came close to doing so in the case of Cecil Beaton's parents who had a butler called Loynes. For your

15

future consideration may I suggest some names that simply breathe distinction and reliability, such as Bulstrode, Purkiss, Thirkettle and Keeping. Or, in the world of monosyllables, Crump, Bloor and Poole.

It seems that already 98 would-be butlers have applied for admission to the Belair Academy. Incidentally, I note a tendency to call butlers 'Jeeves', but Jeeves was a personal man-servant in sole charge of his employer and was therefore a gentleman's gentleman. He would not be slow to point out that he was thus of a slightly superior standing, though the point is debatable.

And with the success of the butler course, who can doubt that a sister-school for British parlourmaids will be rapidly set up? Here again the theatre reminds us of their particular role in life. At the rise of the curtain they are 'discovered' answering the telephone and saying 'Her ladyship is not back yet, Madam'. Later on they answer it again, this time adding 'Ah, I think I hear her car now', an indication that the star of the piece is about to make her entrance.

And for the rest, they fend off the amorous attentions of the young son of the house ('Oh do give over, sir! I've got my job to consider'). They make great play with feather dusters, ceaselessly dusting dustless surfaces. They bring in tea. They are invariably pretty, and in farces they rush in and out, screaming rather a lot.

In course of time, butlers may even eclipse Stilton cheese and Scotch as being our most characteristic and valuable export. It appears that the going rate for a British butler in America is about £10,000 a year, and service in Britain is only rated slightly less, with free board and lodging thrown in, an immensely welcome perk. Doubtless parlourmaids' emoluments are on an equally lavish scale, and quite right too.

Well, I'm seriously thinking of putting in my application to Dulwich, bolstered up with whatever I can think of in the way of extra attractions. 'Has some French' and 'Said to be good mixer' might do. As a sense of dedicated and sober purpose is clearly the thing to aim at, this isn't perhaps quite the moment for 'Can do passable imitation of Edith Evans'.

WHAT AM I BID?

Who was the sensitive British person who, on visits to Paris, used first of all to take a taxi to the Eiffel Tower and, on arrival, stand immediately beneath the tower for a time, for it was the only spot in the city from which you weren't able to see the unsightly thing?

What a pity that King Kong confined his destructional activities to New York. Let loose in Paris, he would have had M Eiffel's tasteful *chef d'oeuvre* down in half a jiffy, and gobbled up several frogs for good measure.

Ex-schoolboys with an engineering bent would say that from a distance it bears a strong resemblance to one of those splendidly complicated Meccano constructions requiring every item in the set, not to speak of extra boxes of nuts and bolts, complete with a whirring clockwork motor to send the lifts smoothly up and down.

But now, by courtesy of a distinguished Fleet Street journal, comes exciting news. It has been discovered that, like some well-fed prima donna who has been overdoing her farinaceous intake ('Another doughnut, Tosca?'), the Tower is several pounds overweight — a thousand tons of excess and needless metal in fact. No race has a better nose for a bargain than the French and our wily neighbours are planning to strip off the iron superfluities and sell them, at £54 a whack, to eager souvenir collectors.

Those of us who take a keen interest in the public scene cannot have failed to note a recent newspaper announcement to the effect that our ever-hospitable Prime Minister Thatcher gave a lunch party in honour of the Mayor of Paris, a M Quelque-chose, since no name was given. One can only assume that, with two such notabilities meeting, there was the customary 'exchange of gifts' and who can doubt that the Mayor came struggling through the door of No. 10 with an armful of the

17

very first disposable metal joists (they are said to be simply A.1 as paperweights), every one of them hot, so to speak, from the Eiffel Tower.

I have often wondered how good Mrs Thatcher's command of the French language is. What would you think? An O Level with a 'Pass' in Oral? A rather shaky A Level? She would naturally have wished to thank her donor in his own lingo, for which an O Level would have provided something along the lines of *'Merci beaucoup. Quels gentils morceaux de fer!'* An A Level might have afforded a slightly more involved phrase, such as 'Really, Gaston, you oughtn't to have done it', which I think works out as *'Vraiment, Gaston, vous n'auriez pas dû le faire'.*

Then of course came the moment for presenting her reciprocal gift *('Vite, Denis, apporte ici notre quid pro quo')* but what on earth can that have been? An unwanted section of the Albert Memorial? A portion or two of the sadly dismantled Pontings? A few sods, and I speak horticulturally, from Kensington Gardens? Possibly she did not even try to match the Mayor's inspired gift and just settled for a case of a reputable British wine or a whole Stilton *('Pardonnez l'odeur!').*

Once confidently imagines that, with this unexpected windfall of cash coming in, our rapacious friends will hunt about for further profitably saleable items that have hitherto been overlooked. I fear that in this connection there will be those with sufficiently deplorable bad taste to suggest that they could sell off selected portions of Napoleon, and indeed, although wincing at the grisly thought, one does oneself wonder how much his sternum might, if properly advertised and fully authenticated, fetch in the open market.

And, musing along these lines, one cannot help remembering the heart of Louis XIV which, reverently placed on view in London at a public exhibition, was absent-mindedly eaten by a short-sighted clergyman in mistake for a cocktail canapé.

ON THIS DAY

Those responsible for choosing the anniversaries (Assassination of Lincoln) that regularly appear in our daily newspapers (Black Death breaks out and slays millions) don't seem to go out of their way (Massacre at Cawnpore) to cheer us up (Judge Jeffreys opens Bloody Assize).

How lowering it is to be informed, on a wet and chilly morning and after a cascade of accounts rendered has come shooting through the letter-box, that nearly 500 years ago today they were attaching Joan of Arc to the stake and looking round for the matches (and in this connection we can certainly disregard the bad taste 'black' joke that runs 'How do you like your steak, Joan?').

And when not busy depressing us, the anniversary selectors (Deceased Wife's Sister bill passes the Lords) cut out a strong line (Beginning of the Reformation) in boredom and in those statements (Poll Tax established) to which the only possible answer is 'Oh'. And then (Black Hole atrocity) back they go (Charles I beheaded) to the events that they really relish (Suicide of Prince Rudolf) and which they so lavishly provide for the enjoyment of all (Cromwell's body exhumed and hung in chains at Tyburn).

Hardly a year passes without a mention of that happening of which the sole purpose must have been to provide schoolboys with jokes. I refer, of course, to the Diet of Worms, whatever that may have been. Certain names too seem to fascinate our selectors and appear frequently — Robespierre, for example, and Drake and Garibaldi (so difficult to separate him in one's mind from those delicious 'squashed fly' biscuits. Did he perhaps create them? If so, the fact should be clearly stated and credit given).

But not all history has been death and disaster and I would be only too glad to supply a choice of cheery anniversary items for insertion when our own or others' affairs leave something to be desired in the way of agreeable tidings. 'Amusing boating mishap. Venerable Bede gets ducking' conjures up an entirely jolly picture of merry monks splashing about in the shallows way back in dear old 728 A.D. Then what about 'Macbeth Marriage Solemnized. Glamis ceremony well attended. Bride in brown', which would suggest that they had at least a few years of married bliss before any visitors of importance started to arrive, short of a bed, at Inverness ('We've put you in the red room').

Even austere figures of the past could be made, as they travel Life's Highway, to seem (Gladstone cured of painful bunion) a little more (Kaiser's moustache catches fire) like you and me (Opening of Parliament marred. Queen Victoria comes a purler. 'No bones broken' jokes Monarch).

The mention of food always interests and pleases the public and 'Invention of Marzipan' and 'First Fish Finger Eaten' would get the day off to a nice start. Who brought the early doughnuts to England, mashed the first swede and thought of setting pancakes on fire? Informative little factual nuggets of this description are historically vastly preferable to Opening of Manchester Ship Canal, Edward II Murdered in Unusual Fashion, Council of Trent Sits, and Duke of Clarence Upside Down in Butt of Malmsey.

Five hundred years from now, whichever of our present-day occurrences will be considered to warrant an anniversary mention? We now have, so effete have we become, but few beheadings. There is no longer anything to be hoped for from the Black Death. Our kings die in their beds. Nobody is nearly as Venerable as Bede. 'First Man on the Moon' might, I suppose, just make it, coupled with 'Discovery of Penicillin', but that is about it.

But cheer up because, on the other hand, there may well be some fine old muddles as they peruse the dusty headlines of today. 'Wolves Triumphant' gives an alarming picture of animal packs hungrily roaming the Midlands and, at lunchtime, picking off the less fleet of foot. 'England defeats Scotland' will send historians scuttling to libraries for details of this civil war

— the harsh peace terms, confiscation of all whisky stores, the haggis banned.

Whatever will they make of 'Maggie on Her High Horse'? Another plucky Lady Godiva, perhaps? A woman jockey winning the Grand National? Time alone will tell.

Kaiser's moustache catches fire

STRIKE IT RICH

The newspapers seem increasingly to produce maps of the southern coastal regions of England covered in little dots and blobs and lightly and heavily shaded areas, all apparently indicating where oil has been, or will be, or is confidently expected to be, found.

My own Devon area has so far escaped dots and blobs and shaded sections so at the moment we are, commercially, rather out of things. I possess a small parcel of land, four acres at the most, and it contains an orchard bisected by a Dartmoor stream. The orchard provides abundant daffodils, apples and purely decorative trout sometimes as much as four inches long, with attendant heron.

But it also provides a small subsidiary watercourse that at certain periods exudes, in addition to water, a thickish, brownish liquid that, and I say this in no boastful spirit, may well be oleaginous. It is all very exciting and I live in hourly expectation of becoming a blob on one of those informative maps.

This being so, I am busily preparing myself for becoming an oilperson. My Christian name is quite unsuitable for an oil tycoon. Writers of fiction make use of it either for indicating a half-witted booby ('Good old Arthur!'), the butt of the nineteenth hole, or for a tipsy and amorous commercial traveller telling vulgar jokes ('There was this sexy milkman . . .') or chatting up Miss Loosely in the Snug ('Do I see somebody who can manage another port and lemon?').

It is to Hollywood that I have gone for a more fitting Christian name, though as far as I know it has not yet been used and so the copyright is mine. I am calling myself 'Crag'. Crag has a fine, solid, rocky, reliable, weatherbeaten sound. It would go well at board meetings: 'Well, the ball's in your court, Crag': 'We must get Crag's go-ahead on this': 'How say you, Crag?'

And I must hastily acquire a chic wife to host, ghastly verb,

22

the oil baron parties that I shall be throwing and, when not busy hosting, to float about in our pool chest uppermost and displaying shapely mounds. As to her name, I want something shiny and hard and glittering. 'Crystal' seems already to have been used somewhere. 'Steel' would do very well though the phrase 'Steel is just changing her frock in the powder room' might cause political muddles, so I've settled for 'Diamond'. This may get shortened to 'Di' and cause current royal confusion which we must face when the time comes. However, the two names go very well together: 'Oh goody, here come Crag and Diamond!': 'Are you going to Crag and Diamond's "do"?': 'At the Veterans' Ball, methinks I spotted Crag and Diamond Marshall . . .'

The trickiest part of all is going to be to get the lingo exactly right. Technical terms can often be such a bother. When I was young, oil coming out of oil wells was referred to as 'gushing' and so my instinct, after that first successful 'strike' (got it!), will be to ring up friends and cry 'My dear, I'm simply gushing away like a mad thing'. But nobody in *Dallas* ever uses 'gush'. There the modish phrase seems to be 'J.R. is pumping to capacity' (I here refer to his oil activities) and so I shall have to practise saying 'My dear, I am simply pumping away to capacity like a thing possessed'. *Not* as vivid as 'gush', is it? Perhaps when I've cornered the market and ruined everybody else I can go back to gush.

Sacrifices will have to be made. I see that I shall be forced to get rid of a few apple trees to make room for the 'rig' and for the workers I shall plainly have to install some sort of wheeled van buffet (Pete's Eats) and a mobile, six-seater, patented Trundle-Loo Convenience, chemically operated ('In field or city, just sit pretty').

There are still plenty of points to cover. Are empty cider barrels O.K. for oil? Does home-made oil attract VAT? Ought I to be absolutely horrid to Diamond so that she can mutter inaudibly and twitch away like poor old Sue Ellen?

One thing I won't do and that is to wear one of those dotty hats. I should look terribly silly in a ten-gallon and I shall, God knows, be looking already quite silly enough.

CHIPS WITH EVERYTHING

A sadly decreasing number of people can now have seen, for she died in 1956, the marvellous solo sketches performed by the matchless Ruth Draper, among them one called 'Doctors and Diets' in which a brassy New York lady (wasn't her name Mrs Grimmer?) takes three friends to a smart restaurant for lunch, only to find that they are all on diets.

One of them orders a cold boiled turnip. Another a bunch of raw carrots ('Kindly leave the green on'), and the third can only have the juice of eleven lemons — no water or sugar. Mrs Grimmer herself is restricted to three chocolate éclairs.

On the other hand, who could not admire the glorious amplitude and the opulent lines of literature's most famous non-dieter, Empress of Blandings, the Earl of Emsworth's championship pig and one which needed no coaxing to the trough. She resembled, as you may recall, a captive balloon decorated with ears and a tail and was as nearly circular as a pig can get without exploding. Wodehouse describes her as being 'a hearty and even a boisterous feeder'.

Surely, somewhere between Mrs Grimmer's guests and the Empress, happiness must lie, difficult as it is to strike a balance.

At my age, when youthful elasticity of the flesh has gone for ever, if I go to the trouble of losing a pound or two (and trouble it is), there is nothing to, so to speak, take up the slack. Portions of me hang down. Among the various disagreeable-sounding words available in the English language for this hanging down process, among them 'to droop' and 'to flop', the verb 'to sag' really has nothing to recommend it. Nothing nice ever sags. A faulty tennis net sags. An incapably erected marquee sags. Spirits sag. However, sag is what one so indubitably does. Nor has one any say in exactly what part sags. Weight comes off where it will.

With food, it isn't so much the main item that is damaging,

it is what accompanies it. Who can properly enjoy a grilled kipper without toast and butter? What is roast beef when sundered from Yorkshire Pudding or boiled beef without dumplings (there is a plumpish American cabaret artiste who proudly calls herself Miss Baby Dumpling)? Who can fancy sausages without mash? Strawberries would feel insulted unless liberally sprinkled with sugar and then masked, as we in the trade phrase it, with cream.

For those of us who tip the scales at something over twelve stone, it is tempting to think, and to draw comfort from the fact, that plumpness very often leads to happiness. There is much to support this view. Julius Caesar, though later to be so unfortunately involved in a stabbing 'incident', asked to be surrounded by persons who were not thin and who got their regular eight hours a night. Quite so. He knew well enough that fatties aren't going to bother about sticking a dagger into you.

Then contrast, if you will, the miserable-looking figures of El Greco, not a smile to be had, emaciated to a degree, painful to gaze upon and not a superfluous ounce in sight, with the voluptuous lushness of Rubens, so many of whose subjects seem to have forgotten to get dressed again after that invigorating dip. Dimpled chubbiness and merry faces everywhere.

Well, not perhaps quite everywhere. Some of the ladies featured in *The Rape of the Sabines* are looking quite understandably worried — no time to pack ('My dear, I just threw in a toothbrush and a sachet of Lustrene') or to leave a note ('Supper in oven') and a gruelling ride ahead of them. The men, however, wear expressions in which pride of capture and anticipation of fresh friendships are evenly mixed. And their bulging calves and giant biceps and generous *musculature* will obviously be fully equal to the task of hoisting their really enormous female prizes onto the horses.

And while admiring the dainty and concealing wisps of gauze that float about so tastefully among Rubens' naked models, let us spare a sympathetic thought for Mrs Rubens. Catering for her husband must have been quite a little headache. A dish of boiled ham is hardly tactful for somebody who, all morning, has been knee-deep in hams. Ditto roast loin of pork and breast of lamb. Even a leg ('Come dear, another slice?') might be off-putting. I expect she settled for things such as devilled kidneys and poultry — roast duck, possibly. But then roast duck is unthinkable without new potatoes, which is where we came in.

BEDS BY SLEEPWELL

In the good old days of playgoing when theatre programmes cost rather less money and contained rather more information, it was often possible to tell, from the lengthy Acknowledgements section, just what sort of play and performance you were in for.

The acknowledgements ('Cigarettes by Abdulla' has passed into the language) came immediately after the name of the scenery designer, and the designer himself followed details of the scenery that he had so elaborately designed — 'Act III, Scene I, Sir Herbert Bellingham's consulting room. Scene II, the terrace at Medlingham Hall, later that afternoon'. Sometimes there was a note which said 'The curtain will be lowered for a few moments during Act II to denote the passage of several months' and which enabled a stage hand to dart on and change vases of sweet peas to vases of chrysanthemums.

In the light comedy 'vehicles' in which Marie Tempest, Lilian Braithwaite and Yvonne Arnaud so joyously and profitably appeared, the management expressed gratitude, as well they might, to the providers of grand pianos, chandeliers, 'silverware', fur coats, champagne, flowers, cigars, flowered cretonnes, table lighters, pocket lighters, jewels and other signs of *de luxe* living, for one associated these three great stars with nothing less, though Dame Lilian preferred to be in a more interesting play when she could find one.

But there was an exception to these outpourings of thanks. In those days (and I don't know what happens now) the plays of Shakespeare were put on with no acknowledgements at all. One hunted in vain for managements to show proper appreciation of Cleopatra's asps ('kindly supplied by Reptiles Inc.'), Gertrude's closet curtains ('from a design by Blanche Westinghouse'), Richard III's hump ('inflatable cushion by Inflatable Cushions') and much else besides — Hamlet's poisoned goblet,

27

the garlands in *Henry VIII*, Portia's caskets. Not one admiring word for a single one of them.

And here one's thoughts turn yet again to Lady Macbeth. How much more vivid and gripping the sleep walking scene would be if one only knew in advance that her apricot night-dress and feathered mules were the creation of Slumbertyte Bedwear. And in those early scenes which reveal her as the con-scientious and deeply caring housewife (her question to her husband about the length of Duncan's stay — '. . . and when goes hence?' — merely shows that she is wondering whether the venison will go round twice), the knowledge that she is kitted sartorially out by 'Tweedily' of Tweed House, Berwick-on-Tweed would mean much. And while we're at it, whence, may one ask, Banquo's kilt? Any sensible management will rely, for all the knives that *Macbeth* needs, on the 'Sheffo' Luxi-kut range, and will have them cleaned nightly with Goddards.

No programme ever said it, but who can doubt that the cauldron of which the three witches made such splendid culinary use came from Jumbo Kitchenware ('Big is Beauti-ful'), of Steam House, Staines? The ladies are busily making, you'll recall, what seems to be an early type of *bouillabaisse*, con-taining, as it does, newts, frogs, shark fillets and lizards, all generously seasoned and spiced. Harrods could probably help here. Mention is also made of a pilot's thumb. Whether the pilot's thumb went also into the soup we do not know, so cut, if you'll forgive it, the thumb.

Many programmes say thank you for 'a gas stove kindly lent by the North Thames Gas Board'. 'Lent' you note! Mean even then, and one pictures them gathering round the stage door on the last night and clamouring anxiously for their stove. Perhaps if it had been the Inverness one they wouldn't have dared to ask Lady Macbeth, prone to fits of violence, for it back.

GILDING THE LILY

I am not quite sure to what extent the admirable Dutch army is involved in any European defence of the west but we can all have quiet confidence in the splendour of their military appearance for, in addition to the hair-nets and long hair that they have been allowed to have since the 1960s, I see that they are now to be permitted to sport ear-rings.

I am informed that the decision on what further items of jewellery they may wear (one's thoughts instantly fly to privates covered in diamanté butterflies and sergeants with diamond clips) will be announced later. Although there seems here to be a risk of 'painting the lily' and one wonders whether too many rings may not painfully chafe the fingers when firing from the hip, I do see that freshly waved hair caught up in a snood, with a pearl or ruby here and there, does bring a new interest to the battlefield.

I have to confess, and to my shame, to possessing only a very limited knowledge of Holland. Delightful though I am certain the country is, I have usually only just passed through by rail or car when on the way to somewhere else. There are, I know, windmills and wind. There are dykes. There is a racy-sounding resort called Bergen-op-Zoom and there was once a flying Dutchman who sang rather a lot. There are gentlemen with patched trousers and clogs and there is a very great deal of water.

Some time ago I hoped to widen a little the extent of my Dutch knowledge by attending a performance of a musical of yesteryear called *Miss Hook of Holland*, not, of course, the original production in 1907 but a tasteful revival at Daly's Theatre in 1932.

The first act was set in a Cheese Market on the very shores of the Zuyder Zee, and the second in a liqueur distillery (Foreman: Ludwig Schnapps), and I was therefore able to add both cheese and heady spirits to my treasure-chest of Dutch availabilities, but apart from those, ascertainable facts were sadly sketchy. The plot, which needn't worry us overmuch, concerned the missing recipe for Mr Hook's most famous and profitable liqueur and there was a merry musical number sung by a lady whose admirers gave her, of all indelicate tributes, petticoats:

> I've a little pink petty from Peter,
> And a little blue petty from John.
> And I've one green and yellow
> From some other fellow,
> And one that I haven't got on.

But of the Dutch language itself, not one word was spoken, and here I am still in difficulties for a jolly friend whose bona fides I do not fully trust assures me that the Dutch word of command for 'Mount!' in the days when they had cavalry and horses was 'Skramble op de beeste'. Improbable, I agree with you, and to this he has added what may well be misinformation to the effect that 'Don't Walk on the Grass' comes out as 'Nit Brillen in de Buschen', and that when *Hamlet* is performed, the Ghost's line, 'I am thy father's spirit', reaches the public as 'Ik ben de Poppaspook'. Unlikely again but on the other hand, and please forgive any misremembered spellings, I have myself seen Helpmann's superb ballet, *Miracle in the Gorbals*, transformed on an Amsterdam poster into 'Het Wunder in de Schloppen'.

Ace crossword solvers, skilful at the anagrams on which these puzzles so often rely, will be able to work out the fact that 'Het' corresponds to our English 'The', and elsewhere all seems plain sailing with 'pen' meaning pen and 'sap' meaning sap and 'kat' easily identifiable as cat.

A trap awaits one, however, in the form of the noun 'kikker'. Football is clearly involved, one supposes, although the English verb 'to kick' has become a dirty word, apart, alas, from occasional activities on the terraces and commentators prefer to say that 'he struck the ball' or, in more flowery fashion, 'he powered the ball into the net'. And so 'kikker', one imagines, is what I, in my stuffy old way, would refer to as 'centre-forward' or, possibly, 'left-half'.

Not at all. 'Kikker' means, of all things, 'frog' and rightly belongs in quite another country, ratty though ardent Francophiles may get when one refers to the inhabitants as such.

REST AWHILE

Many of us whose occupations require us to travel from time to time about the country and stay in hotels, regret the proliferation of the modern and New Look hotel, often part of a chain, whose proprietors' main idea is that you should spend the major part of your time in your bedroom, comforted by the presence there of TV, telephone, drinks dispenser and DIY tea-maker with that milk that isn't nearly as nice as fresh milk.

Although hotel guide writers try to bump up the charms of these places with some such sentence as 'At the pre-prandial hour we were privileged to join Mine Host and his good lady, Topsy Tregunter-Scott, for a cheery aperitif in the Tudor Bar', the bar turns out to be postage-stamp size and about as Tudor as a space module. The downstairs amenities are few and the lifts encourage one to ascend to an upstairs anti-social isolation.

One longs for the old-fashioned country town hotel. No revolving-door here but an entrance hall embellished with potted palms and handsomely-framed and fly-blown photographs of yesteryear's politicians (Mr Baldwin looking reliable) which leads into a spacious and arm-chaired area, with a grandfather clock stopped at some unlikely hour and a wide mahogany reception desk with a notice saying KINDLY RING FOR MANAGERESS.

The bell for ringing with is one of those brass ones that you bang sharply on the head and its metallic 'Ping' brings into view, after a suitable pause, a stately presence, the Manageress in person emerging from some fusty hinterland and prepared to be graciousness itself ('Room 14 commands a view of our herbaceous border. We rather pride ourselves on our border!').

As with those of us who sometimes appear, seated, on television, it is only the top halves of Manageresses that are ever seen as they come gliding forward and on the decoration of their top halves they do not spare themselves. Lustrous satin blouse in a pastel shade, floral spray pinned to generous bosom, strings of pearl-type pearls and flashing smile — all is firmly in position, together with a resplendent coiffure whose loops and coils and curls lead one to think that not all of it can, in the very nature of things, be home-grown. Of what can their invisible bottom halves consist? An old tweed skirt, perhaps, and a pair

It is only the top halves of Manageresses that are ever seen

of stout golfing brogues? Something sensible and comfy, anyway.

One registers and notes that among one's fellow residents are Colonel and Mrs Slowly-Jones (of Fairways, Godalming), with whom social contact is gradually established — the exchange of polite bows on the way into dinner, the 'good morning' at breakfast, the chance encounter outside Boots ('Ah, we meet again!'), the pooling of views on current news items ('Would you care for a peep at my *Mail*?'), the whispered culinary advice at lunch ('I can recommend the Cabinet Pudding') and the cementing of the relationship as we all gather round the telly in the first floor lounge (Residents Only), where the chairs are often all against the wall as though the centre of the room had been cleared for a wild knees-up-Mother-Brown.

If one didn't know already for whom the New Look hotels are primarily intended, the eager enquiry at the desk of 'Which firm are you with?' would tell you, but now it seems that all is no longer *couleur de rose*. I am told, and my informant is none other than a spokesman for the world's biggest hotel chain, Holiday Inn, that a snag of an unexpected kind has appeared. Businessmen, heavy with the cares of the commercial world, are also heavy with expense account breakfasts, 'working lunches' and vast dinners and their weight is playing Old Harry with the sides of the beds on which they plonk themselves in order to telephone. 'Hullo, hullo, is that Bagshaw's?' is followed all too often by an ominous creaking of springs, a sadly sagging mattress, and there has had to be an expensive re-think of Holiday furnishings and bedroom arrangements in order to site the businessmen ('Is that Hoggit and Bumfield?') elsewhere than on the bed while telephoning.

No such problems exist in country town hotels for the sole telephone is in the charge of the Manageress. However, another ping on her bell brings her smoothly out, prepared to connect you urgently with Barnstaple and all ready, cheerfully hoping for Something Sensational, to listen to every word.

THIS LITTLE PIG

One summer's day in the mid-Thirties I found myself, at that time a schoolmaster, in a fortune-teller's tent at what was then called, and perhaps still is, a Fun Fair. I had been enticed within by a placard outside that said, possibly rather equivocally, MADAME OLGA REVEALS ALL, Madame shyly adding, in rather small letters, that knowledge of what the mysterious future held for them would cost her clients half-a-crown a whack.

Madame Olga turned out to be a gloomy, brooding presence, much done up gypsy-fashion with a good many clanking bracelets and who, after some preliminary questioning (age, profession, favourite colour), settled to her task. She closed her eyes, breathed heavily, seemed to go off into a sort of mini-trance (a full trance, I imagined, would be 6d extra) and then said, in a dreamy voice, 'I see paper'.

'And you're not the only one, dear' was my witty rejoinder, remembering the sixty or so French exercises that I would have to correct and mark on my return to school, but in the fortune-telling world back-chat was plainly not encouraged for Madame became huffy and sulky, muttered, not forgetting to keep in character and a trouper to the last, 'You 'ave broken ze spell' and our interview was at an end. I was too polite to ask for a refund and decided to write my 2s 6d off as Experience.

One of the occupational risks of schoolmastering is death by suffocation under a giant mound of paper and therefore those in the teaching profession will be less horrified than others by the appalling statistics recently made public and concerning the EEC Commission's prodigal use of paper. A London Labour Euro-MP, Mr Lomas, has discovered that the Common Market produces every year sufficient unnecessary documents to cover a cricket pitch to a depth of more than 500 feet, which is a whole lot of feet too many.

Aware that not all readers, alas, are cricket buffs and wanting, in my clumsy way, nobody to be left out, I have asked a kind mathematician friend to bring the facts home to one and all by estimating the depth of documents on playing areas in other games with which most will be familiar. And thus we find that a tennis court would have 31 feet of documents, a rugger pitch 7, a croquet lawn 10 and a table tennis table 1,467 feet, or about a quarter of a mile of paper.

Mr Lomas, a force for good if ever I saw one and a man rightly rattled by this yearly wastage in money of well over three million pounds, has placed his findings before Mrs Thatcher and M Gaston Thorne, President of the Brussels EEC Commission, and between the two of them they may, furnished with the above disquieting facts, be able to achieve sensational reductions in cash, time and waste in the matter of paper.

One would, I think, hardly care to be the Commission's President, plushy though I don't doubt the conditions and rewards of employment are. For one thing, one would have to know how to say 'Oh *do* stop squabbling!' in at least seven different European languages and once again in these pages I am at a loss to know whatever 'stop squabbling' would come out as in Dutch.

What a pity that I am no longer a schoolmaster teaching French. A number of interesting examination sentences for translating into French spring to mind.

Beginners
  1 Is this the market?   Why is everybody so cross?
  2 I am not happy here.   It is not nice.   Let us go home.
  3 The Channel is choppy *(clapoteuse)* and very useful.

O Level
  1 Are these truly your most popular apples? What a sorry lot!
  2 François hates Heinrich, but they both hate James much more.

3 These are our fish! Kindly remove your nets at once.

A Level
  Write not more than 200 words of French on the
  following:
  'It is not true to say that the more you put into a thing, the
  more you get out'.

BY PROFESSION

In the field of fiction, dramatic or otherwise, dentists and doctors and, I need hardly add, veterinary surgeons, play roles of increasing importance and frequency and many of them have become, and how rightly, darlings of the public. What figures of awe or alarm or admiration the mere names conjure up — Dr Jekyll, Dr Clitterhouse, Dr Watson, Dr Lakington (popped, you'll recall, into that acid bath by Bulldog Drummond), Dr Findlay, and that doctor of Shaw's who had such a very memorable and profitable Dilemma.

Anything concerning illness, death and bovine disaster is indeed stirring stuff, and in the practice of dentistry an impacted wisdom tooth requiring extraction ('A little wider, please') is a matter that holds the attention ('Now rinse'), though there isn't, perhaps, much dramatic mileage to be got out of the correct use of dental floss.

One's heart goes out therefore to those involved in professions or occupations woefully neglected by writers and dramatists and on which the limelight never plays. There they sit or, in the case of bus conductors, stand, longing for their moment of glory, their chance to be a hero.

Picture, if you will, the busy high street of a county town. It is midday, peak hour for shoppers, and suddenly a Mrs Huxtable puts a hand to her bosom and lets out a cry of anguish. Her patented Karribag trolley, 'the purchasers' pal', has lost a wheel, has spilled her parcels onto the pavement, and her 'on offer' Garibaldis and her 'sell by May 14th' yoghurt are in danger of being trampled underfoot.

What is to be done? Everybody is staring aghast at the stricken woman when suddenly, from a neighbouring block of offices, a male form dashes out, deftly replaces the wheel and scoops up Garibaldis and yoghurt cartons. 'Who are you?' admiring onlookers ask. 'A doctor? A dentist? Possibly a veterinary surgeon?' 'I am none of these fine things', the hero replies. 'I am an average-adjuster. I adjust', he adds, not wishing to appear boastful but anxious to make everything quite clear, 'averages. I was busy adjusting when I heard this lady's desperate cry and so I put down my pen and . . .' — but the crowd has melted, disappointed, away, and even Mrs Huxtable has ungratefully removed herself and her rescued Garibaldis.

Who can doubt that the same wounding treatment would be handed out to, say, Damp Proof Consultants, Ball-Bearing Stockists, Roofing Contractors, Abattoir Assistants, Vending Machine Suppliers, and the 'Loppo' Tree-Felling Agency ('Branches everywhere')?

Sometimes a subterfuge may be resorted to in order to conceal the lack of a romantic profession. Picture, and again if you will, a crowded Covent Garden opera house waiting for a gala performance of Buffo's *La Costiva*. The lights lower and a figure edges out from between the curtains bringing with it dire news. Consternation! The great tenor, Signor Blotti, has a chest cold and cannot sing the exacting role of Constipato.

There is horror on every face, but what is this? A member of the audience hastily rises and rushes backstage, face alight and breathing fast. 'I will sing Constipato', he cries. 'In my youth I studied in Milano under Potti and am word and note perfect'. 'But who are you?' they demand. 'I am Ernest Merryweather and I am a costings clerk.' 'Hush, hush, for pity's sake lower your voice', they answer. A hurried consultation and then the exciting decision. 'You can forget all that costings stuff. From now on you are Signor Dotti, a retired Italian dentist. Tog up, and somebody go and tell the orchestra to get on with the overture.'

I am not without experience in the matter of unromantic professions. Renewing, a few years ago, my passport, and being required to name my calling, I wrote, rather pleased with myself, the word WRITER. But my writing was not as clear as it might be and the passport returned to me with my profession described as WAITER. I can assure you, from my experiences at frontiers and airports, that waiters do not, alas, rank very highly in the public mind.

MASTER BEETON

Before I pass on to an important educational theme, may I be allowed to add just one more to the list I gave you of Useful Facts for setting conversational balls rolling. This one is to the effect that Rupert Brooke had prehensile toes and could pick up a tennis ball with his foot.

What a boon this must have been during lax play on that Cambridgeshire tennis court when a badly flighted lob cleared the stop-netting and landed with a plop in the Grantchester mere, with the church clock standing, by then, at four-fifteen, a less easy figure to find something to rhyme with it. Rupert (was he ever 'Rupe' in unbuttoned moments?) had just to stick a leg into the water to retrieve it.

He could also, I am informed, seize a match with one foot and the match-box with the other and then strike a light, an achievement (I nearly wrote 'feat') the usefulness of which is not too immediately apparent. Perhaps, great lover as he was, it came in handy when a lady was entwined in his arms and he suddenly felt the urge to smoke what was then, and by many, merrily referred to as 'a gasper', a word before its time in under-lining the undoubted dangers and results of indulgence in the fragrant weed.

But now to the agitating question that has recently been uppermost in everybody's mind, namely how suitable is it that, during 'equal opportunities' lessons at a Merseyside co-educational school, a boy of 13 should be encouraged to bake a batch of fairy cakes, subsequently being allowed to take the toothsome *gâteaux* home for the appreciation and enjoyment of his parents.

How charmingly the little scene would have gone in Victorian times:

He could also . . . seize a match in one foot . . . and then
strike a light

'What have you there, Edwin?'

'Why, fairy cakes, Papa. I baked them specially for you and Mama, the schoolmaster aiding me'.

'Capital, capital!'

'I burnt my finger on the oven door but said a prayer to Him Who Knoweth All and did not weep'.

'What appetising comestibles. Let us call Mama. Emily, my dear, pray cease your tatting and join us here in the conservatory'.

But the Merseyside father was far from being a Victorian one and it seems that the scene went rather less successfully, the idea of boys who love games and other manly pursuits learning to cook being described as 'ludicrous', a point of view which is quite understandable.

I rather wonder whether, in this context, the somewhat unfortunate word 'fairy' did not do some additional damage and create unease, while our imagined scene might have gone, in the present day, a bit better with a different and robuster-sounding cooked article:

'What have you got there, Dean?'

'A great wodge of plum duff, Dad. Bags of jam and piping hot'.

'Good for you, son. Let's all get stuck in. Hi, Syl, come on down. That school's done something sensible at last'.

Other dishes that could make an unhappy impression on fathers might be apple turnovers and queen of puddings. And I wouldn't myself be too totally confident about puff pastry.

Modern mothers, ever practical and less easily fussed than their husbands, seem likely to take an altogether rosier view of their sons' culinary activities and abilities. Now that cookery is a recognised examination subject, one can picture the excited telephone calls and exchange of news. 'Cynthia? My dear, you remember Julian's super O Level in game pies and fig *surprise*? Well, the darling boy has decided to go on to his A Level and he's now "into" *coq au vin* and stuffed marrows. It's too wonderful. I don't ever have to go *near* the kitchen. He does it all.'

All must, however, agree that the ever-widening curricula in schools is a Good Thing in a country where a century ago it was the Classics and little else. For many years now a splendidly go-ahead public school called Oundle has been casting its net wide in the scholastic sea. Happily educated there as I was, you may be astounded to know that at the age of 14 I was taught how to shoe a horse. Every term we spent a week either at lathes and fashioning metal objects, or at benches doing ditto with wood. There was a foundry spitting molten stuff, and a forge. The horses to be dealt with were mostly the cart kind and leant on one in a friendly manner. It is some years now since I last shoed a horse but I dare say that the old skill is still there. If you're in difficulties with dear old Dobbin, just bring him along.

WHO DID YOU SAY?

Gazing as one does, and in considerable awe, at the entries in *Who's Who*, I sometimes feel as though the sole purpose of some of the blameless lives therein enshrined has been, so suitable and characteristic are they, to get themselves included in that noble volume.

Turning its pages, one is struck again and again by the vast number of persons of obvious importance whom one does not know and of whom one has hitherto never heard. There they have been, beavering away in Life's Logpiles on our and their own behalf and with never a grateful word or a sign of recognition from the general public.

What, for example, about Sir Chapland Forster-Browne, and though I am here describing a fictional character, I cannot add the well-worn words 'any resemblance to any living person is purely coincidental' because the resemblance to most *Who's Who* persons is the whole point.

Everything about Sir Chapland ('Chappie' to fellow R.A.C. members) is as it should be. He was *b* in 1910 — and I will translate the italicised letters for the benefit of the uninitiated — which means that he was born in 1910, a thing that might happen to anybody. He was *Educ.* (yes indeed, educated, or at least that's what it claims) at Dumbleton and Oxford, *m* (married) in 1934 Priscilla Evelyn Maud, sixth daughter (and one can almost see the despair on the parents' faces) of the Hon. Jasper and Mrs Neddycotte, *q.v.* (which is *quod vide* and is Latin, or so I believe, for 'which see' and reveals that Jasper's details too are somewhere available). 'Two *s*, one *d*' indicates that the Forster-Browne union has been blessed to the tune of three children, the sexes of which are clear to all.

Career outlines then appear. 'Followed his father into the family firm of Culshaw and Merridew and is author of *In The Stocks*, a light-hearted account of City life between the wars.'

44

And then it is chairman of this and director of that, and 'took a keen interest in our far-eastern jute connections and sat on the Advisory Council' (and when we say 'sat on', we mean sat on in two senses, one of them rather less pleasant than the other).

Finally comes the address, often in Surrey and always inspiring utter confidence — Great Clinkers, Meadowlands, near Guildford, and it conjures up a gracious picture of semi-country life, with its croquet lawn, sun-drenched loggia, barbecue, heated pool and garaging for five cars with chauffeur's accommodation what is known as 'over'.

Not all entries include information about Recreations and it is hard to know what, in this case, to put, for Sir Chapland's chief recreation has been to be perfectly beastly to almost everybody. However, doubtless he would play for safety and we read 'Golf and Gardening', both of them totally reputable occupations. The recreation section gives a chance for the whimsical and joky entry: 'Minding my own business' perhaps, or dear old 'Messing about in boats'. But, on the whole, grim respectability is here the thing to aim at and I append a list of activities for you when your turn comes, to choose from — walking, badminton, hunting, fishing, travel, bee-keeping, painting. Choose not more than three, for an excess of recreation implies frivolity and looks bad in these sober pages.

Might I suggest to the publishers of this indispensable reference book that an occasional homely detail would make the names and careers seem a little more human. How about, after *m*, 'and what a mistake *that* was!'? 'One *d*' is really very dull, so why not add on 'a cheerful girl called Tracylou who works at a stables and looks more and more like a rather jolly horse'. Well then, 'two *s*' would greatly increase in interest with 'both of them *Educ.*, like Dad, at Dumbleton — one expelled and the other "asked to leave"'. A list of the clubs from which Sir Chapland had been blackballed should be added to the list of clubs unwise enough to welcome him in. Little touches like that would be much more in keeping with Life's light and shade and the warp (I'll say) and woof of existence.

Obviously at their wits' end for space-fillers, the publishers have recently included the present writer. I seem, rightly, just as humdrum and ordinary as all the others. When it came to recreations, I wanted to put 'Envy, Sloth, Gluttony, Greed and Sin in general', but I played for safety ('Reading and sitting in the sun') just like everybody else.

OLD SCHOOL TIES

The surprising sight, in a recent episode of *Dallas*, of J.R. wearing what was obviously an Old Etonian tie, will have proved very reassuring to those among us who have, in our sympathetic way, been worrying quite a lot about the scholastic and formative backgrounds and the moral attitudes of some of those high up in the American oil world, and J. R. Ewing in particular.

Ever since that poor girl, who took the famous pot shot at him and made the bookmakers a fortune, plunged to her watery death while in close proximity to J.R., one hasn't been, well, quite *happy* about him. Now, however, all is changed for who can doubt that the values instilled in him by that splendid old Berkshire school will, in due course and late in the day though it already is, come shining through.

It is far from easy to find out J.R.'s age but I estimate him to be somewhere down the wrong end of the thirties so that he would have been at Eton from about 1957 to 1961, fertile years indeed. How pleasing to imagine the chubby youngster arriving as a new boy complete with, indeed, an Eton collar, too much pocket-money and one of those jackets that used to be saucily called bum-freezers. Alighting from the train at Slough and on the way to Windsor by bus, he doubtless tried, before the high moral tone of Eton had got into him, to interest his fellow pupils in the purchase of shares in a mythical oil-field in the Texan outback, prior to softening up Matron with a gift of liqueur chocs ('You're wasted here, Miss Battersby. Now, my Daddy owns this night-club . . . .').

The ease and grace with which J.R. instantly and instinctively struck out for the side, when recently pushed by an angry half-sister-in-law into the South Fork swimming-pool, clearly shows him to have been a wet-bob and therefore fully familiar with the Eton Boating Song, with its emphasis on rhythmical and essentially corporate action and a selfless absence of individuality while rowing. Such fine seeds sown must, in the end, bear fruit, and the song's lines about 'swinging together' will have struck no jarring note at a time when capital punishment was, mercifully, no more.

In another field, I am anxious, and perhaps rather more than I need to be, about Lady Macbeth. Readers will recall the sadly wasted opportunities there. Whatever can have been her schooling? Although one now hears that such establishments are productive forcing-grounds of talent and veritable temples of decency and decorum, one seems to see her, pig-tails flying and a victim of the distressing acne that seemed to be so much a part of growing up, at a rather tough comprehensive in, say, Ross and Cromarty. I picture her as a vigorous hockey captain (Cries of 'Sticks!') and a regular demon at the bully-off, and with, in her last years, A Levels in Sociology and the Culinary Arts (Distinction in the paper on 'How To Carve'). Although her final term's report contained the age-old phrase 'We are sorry to see her go', the sighs of relief could have been comfortably heard in Aberdeen.

How very different if she had been entered for Roedean, with the balmy and beneficial South Coast air working its customary magic and with 'Dr Brighton' just round the corner. There any extravagant and ambitious tendencies, especially regal ones, would have been gently checked by the headmistress ('Aren't we getting a weeny bit above ourselves, dear?') while a mug of steaming cocoa last thing would have ensured a lifetime's habit of restful slumber, not to speak of restful slumber too for anyone in the spare room.

As for Ophelia, I rather fear that she was 'educated privately', those useful words that in biographical sketches sometimes cover scholastic inadequacies, for she seems to be a frail and wispy little thing, woefully lacking in intellectual powers. Where she learnt those licentious verses, who can say? Here again, Roedean would have been the answer. No such verses there, and, being so near the sea, they would at least have taught her how to swim.

MANY THANKS

It seems that those who take their holidays patriotically on England's bright and breezy South Coast are in for an interesting biological experience. From faraway Japan and borne on who knows what marine currents there has floated to our shores the *Sargassum muticum*, a prolific seaweed which, like many a human, particularly enjoys the cheerful amenities of Bournemouth, Brighton and Eastbourne and can even be found happily waving its tendrils as far west as Mousehole.

Although it is inedible and not much use chemically as a fertilizer, I am glad to congratulate the Japanese on having invented it for I recently got into bad trouble with Sweden for drawing attention to what I considered to be their somewhat modest contributions (Swedish drill and mashed swedes) to this world's more useful benefits. For now a loyal, and inedible, Swede has sent me a long list of that country's proud national achievements, among their discoveries being oxygen, dynamite, ball bearings and 'the high-speed pneumatic dental drill' (er, thank you). And to cap all, no fewer than seven craters on the moon bear the names of Swedish scholars. Phew!

And so, before other countries start to feel out of things and begin to complain, let us scatter grateful acknowledgements far and wide. Schoolboys would certainly wish me to mention French cricket, that joyous and simple variant where the batsman's legs form the stumps (such a welcome saving in financial outlay) and the whole game is over in ten minutes. This is not the place perhaps for mentioning that unauthorised form of departure known as taking French leave, or certain other French matters. A friendly wholesomeness is what we are here after.

Well then, who, gazing at one of France's near neighbours, plucky little Belgium, does not instantly see in the mind's eye a steaming pile of nutritional fragrance, a dish of freshly cooked

Brussels sprouts, the miniature cabbage in all its glory, each one forming the most succulent of *bouchées*. A word of praise therefore for this tenderly nurtured Walloon comestible, so skilfully grafted, or whatever it is that new vegetables require.

As to another of France's neighbours, although the popular song goes 'I miss my Swiss, my Swiss miss misses me', Swiss misses, however attractive, can hardly be listed as a valuable national invention on a par with safety matches (yes, Sweden again) and so here we must limit our thanks to the ingeniously contrived Swiss roll which, liberally dusted with caster and lavishly jammed, is such a welcome addition to the tea-table.

It is interesting to note that, first things first and human nature being what it is, food in various forms is what we often think of in connection with this or that country. What tastes better than Irish stew? Who, wishful to munch at home, would dream of taking away anything that wasn't Chinese? Up in Scotland they have, tastefully enshrined in a sausage-meat jacket, hard-boiled eggs, such a boon to picnickers. The Welsh have their rabbits (or rarebits to the know-alls). What goulash is lusher than the Hungarian kind?

Here and there a feebleness reveals itself, poor old sunny Italy just having to settle for having provided the world with Roman noses. The Egyptians merely have their dear old mummies to cherish and the Greeks have their urns, but with them the pleasing responsibility for 'What's a Greek urn?', a jolly music-hall joke of the old-fashioned kind, the answer being 'About thirty bob a week'.

To the south-west of Europe, the picture is altogether a less agreeable one. When we think of Spain, it is not Spanish onions that spring first to mind but Spanish tummy. And Portugal may indeed be our oldest ally (and you have to go pretty far back to find them lending a hand) but their men-of-war were not of the kind to be very helpful in the last conflict.

And what, you may well ask, of Holland? They provide Double Dutch and even the merest nodding acquaintance with their language will tell you why.

LINGER LONGER DO

At the end of a London dinner given in his honour and celebrating his seventieth birthday, Somerset Maugham found himself reluctantly upon his feet and making a speech in the course of which he stated that it was a well known fact that considerable solaces and comforts were attached to the process of growing old.

His listeners, many of them fairly ancient, leant eagerly forward, anxious to be solaced and comforted, only to find Mr Maugham, after a lengthy silence, announcing that he couldn't now for the life of him remember what any of the alleged solaces and comforts were.

He should be alive today when a caring government (oh yes it is) lavishes benefits upon the elderly, of which I am one, and it is with a full and grateful heart that I read that an official ukelele player, encouraged by a Government grant of £40 a week, is to bring musical joy to old age pensioners in old people's homes in, I note, the Norfolk area. Oh hooray! What could be better? One is tempted to up-anchor immediately and hasten to the Wash.

I am never quite clear just what the difference, if any, is between a ukelele and a banjo, both of which seem to require vigorous twanging, but as regards the former, some readers' memories and minds will have gone happily back to the 1920s and to a tuneful and lively ditty called 'Ukelele Lady', first heard in a spirited rendering in a London revue.

The song's verse now escapes me but the chorus began strongly with a delightful promise of mutual affection:

> 'If you like a Ukelele Lady,
> Ukelele Lady like-a you.'

Let me at once clear up an important point, namely the sex of the 'you' in lines 1 and 2. In my articles I have always set my

An official ukelele player . . . is to bring musical joy to
old age pensioners

face against any form of immodesty and have declared my section of the page to be a No Go Area for unconventional thoughts, and it is clear that the 'you' here refers to a male person and not to one lady admiring another lady, with or without a ukelele.

One seems to see the instrumentalist as being dusky and sporting hibiscus blossoms in her hair. Although I have in my Devon garden no fewer than three hibiscus bushes which make light of the worst of the frosts and every year throw out a profusion of flowers, I cannot picture the Lady among, say, the palms of Torquay or on Paignton's spacious beaches, however sultry the SW weather conditions. I seem to see her against a background of coconuts — Hawaii perhaps.

With lines 3 and 4 of the lyric, difficulties arise. They run, and I write from memory,

> 'If you like to linger where it's shady,
> Ukelele Lady linger too.'

The bold statement is rather shocking and the introduction of the word 'shady' is unfortunate in the extreme, though it rhymes with 'Lady' and here means 'in the shade'. However 'shady' has about it such a hint of disreputable conduct that I suggest that, in the event of your trying the song yourself, you just mumble 'shady', secure in the knowledge that mumbling is quite a feature of some pop singers' performances. Perhaps they are shy about trotting out lyrics that are not always in the topmost class.

If, as I hope, the Norfolk songbird includes the number in his repertoire as a special treat for lady pensioners, the words are quite easy to adapt. The opposite of Lady is Gentleman which, as it has three syllables, must be shortened to two, giving us

> 'If you like a Ukelele Genty,
> Ukelele Genty like-a you.'

Rhymes for Genty are hardly numerous. The writer, G. A. Henty, must be at once ruled out, even though he must be one of the very few authors to die tied up — I am speaking nautic-

ally — on his very own yacht in Weymouth harbour.
However, I am happy to suggest

'If you munch coconuts a-plenty,
Ukelele Genty munch-a too.'

Pop groups seem to appear increasingly often upon the telly
and I try, in my hopeless old way, to take an interest. Are those
instruments they use ukeleles? Banjos, perhaps? Guitars, possibly? The performers prance and twang and shriek and jig up
and down while the lights (a fresh menace) flash on and off and
one's senses reel. Can they perhaps be trying to take one's mind
off the thinnish nature of the song? Could be.

RING FOR
OUR BOOTS

RING FOR OUR BOOTS

How often do we quote Doctor Watson, but how sadly few are the details about him that we can call to mind. We remember his indignant outbursts and his cry of 'Good Heavens, Holmes! This is intolerable', on hearing that their rooms at 221b Baker Street have been set on fire by Professor Moriarty. We remember his tendency ('My head is in a whirl') to be somewhat easily baffled. We remember, of course, his firm grasp of the obvious:

> Sherlock Holmes had not come back yet. It was nearly ten o'clock before he entered, looking pale and worn. He walked up to the sideboard, and, tearing a piece from the loaf, he devoured it voraciously . . . .
> 'You are hungry', I remarked.

But this cannot be all, and two questions immediately present themselves: Whatever became of Mrs Watson (prominent in *The Sign of Four*), and what, if anything, was Doctor Watson's practice?

Indefatigable as he was in reporting at length over fifty of the cases, Doctor Watson inexcusably excites us by the mention of twenty-two of which we have nothing but the bare names. A little more assiduity and a little less harping on his leg (wounded in the Afghan Campaign and apt to throb in wet weather), and we should have at command such matters as Mrs Farintosh and the Opal Tiara, Ricoletti of the Club Foot and his Abominable Wife, The Singular Affair of the Aluminium Crutch, and The Tragedy of the Atkinson Brothers at Trincomalee. He tantalizes us further with The Vatican Cameos, The Sudden Death of Cardinal Tosca, The Card Scandal at the Nonpareil Club, and The Affair of the Bogus Laundry (the mangles, one supposes, were disguised counterfeiting apparatus). Watson could hardly claim, as you shall see, that marital or professional obligations encroached seriously upon his time. Nor will the plea that some of the cases were complete failures appeal to the amateurs among us; we know the correct methods, then let us apply them to the affair of 'Isadore Persano, the well-known journalist and duellist, who was found stark staring mad with a match-box in front of him which contained a remarkable worm, said to be unknown to science'.

But to Watson's marriage. Despite 'an experience of women which extends over many nations and three separate continents', it is to Lower Camberwell that Doctor Watson comes for his bride and to the house of a Mrs Cecil Forrester. Within is a needy governess with blue eyes, Miss Mary Morstan, attired, for our first view, in 'sombre, greyish beige . . . . and a small turban of the same dull hue'. The Doctor, badly smitten, has 'never looked upon a face which gave a clearer promise of a refined and sensitive nature'. The respectability of Lower Camberwell plays its part in the furthering of the romance:

> As we drove away, I stole a glance back, and I still seem to see that little group on the step — the two graceful, clinging figures, the half-opened door, the hall-light shining through stained glass, the barometer and the bright stair-rods. It was soothing to catch even that passing glimpse of a tranquil English home.

Miss Morstan is similarly enraptured with the Doctor, with his moustache and his square jaw and the Afghan tales which enliven his conversation. Her joy, poor girl, is brief. Her share of the Agra Treasure is dropped, bauble by bauble, into the Thames by Jonathan Small, and after a few months of married life in Paddington ('complete happiness' though it was) the Doctor, hot for Holmes, leaves her repeatedly. Occasionally, before departure, he dashes upstairs to inform her, but once in Baker Street she is totally forgotten. Small wonder that latterly she is often 'away upon a visit' or 'on a visit to her aunt's'. We can but admire her demeanour; loving and dutiful to the end, she fades gradually from the picture, playing graciously into her selfish husband's hands: 'Oh, Anstruther would do your work for you. You have been looking a little pale lately. I think the change would do you good . . .' And so into oblivion, in what manner we do not know, curtly dismissed in a passing reference to 'my recent sad bereavement'.

But, once in Baker Street, what chance would even an experienced charmer have had against the fascinator in the mouse-coloured dressing-gown? The world is well lost indeed when Holmes springs to his feet crying 'Ring for our boots and tell them to order a cab', and off the hansom jingles to Stepney or Covent Garden or Bloomsbury or Holborn or even to Saxe-Coburg Square. There are trips to Croydon, the Cornish Peninsula, Brixton Workhouse, and 'the pretty Surrey village of Esher'. There are thrilling peeps into private houses: The Myrtles, Beckenham: Laburnum Villa, Hammersmith: Briarbrae, Woking. Every call was obediently answered: 'Come at once if convenient', telegraphs Holmes, 'if inconvenient, come all the same', and off scuttles the Doctor, complete with jemmy and dark lantern and chisel, to Goldini's Restaurant, Gloucester Road. London, the outer suburbs and the Southern Counties are the most productive; there appears to have been little serious crime (*The Stockbroker's Clerk*) farther north than Birmingham. Back in Baker Street, with the Borgia jewel deftly prised from the last of the six Napoleon busts, there can be no thought of rest: 'Put the pearl in the safe, Watson', orders Holmes, 'and get out the papers of the Conk-Singleton forgery case'.

A less devoted slave might well have found some of Holmes' habits a little wearing to the nerves. The constant 'ping' of the hypodermic and the frequent snatches upon the violin (a Stradivarius, picked up in the Tottenham Court Road for fifty-five shillings) would perhaps have been bearable if they had been the only idiosyncrasies. They were not. There were the 'weird and often malodorous scientific experiments' and, more alarming, the 'occasional revolver practice within doors'. There were the 'devouring of sandwiches at irregular hours' and the tendency to awaken Watson before dawn on frosty winter mornings (insupportable, even if it meant a trip to Chislehurst). There were the biting of the nails, the times when he 'ran out and ran in', the refusal to make small-talk with the chatty

Doctor, the clouds of the strongest shag tobacco. There was, horror of horrors, a recital at the St James' Hall, with Holmes 'gently waving his long thin fingers in time to the music'.

To offset these failings, Watson had, it must be allowed, much to intrigue him in Holmes' conversation. One's own reminiscences, even when about Afghanistan, are apt to pall and Holmes could hold forth on matters other than crime, passing lightly from severed thumbs to Warships of the Future, from clubbed skulls to the Bertillon System of Measurements, from suffocated peeresses to Miracle Plays. Watson had to learn about The Polyphonic Motets of Lassus and both Mediaeval and Chinese Pottery (including 'the marks of the Hung-wu and the beauties of the Yung-lo and the writings of Tang-ying'). To what extent the good doctor's education had been previously neglected we cannot say. He can bring out a Latin quotation of fourteen words but of his school days we know nothing except that he had been 'intimately associated with a lad named Percy (or "Tadpole") Phelps', nephew of Lord Holdhurst, and that it had been considered piquant to 'chivy him about the playground and hit him over the shins with a wicket'. We can, perhaps, safely assume that Holmes, with his instructive chatter, was not wasting his time. Phelps turns up again at the time of *The Naval Treaty* when Tadpole 'was still weak after his long illness and his misfortunes made him querulous and nervous'. Doctor Watson advances upon the invalid and endeavours (in vain, alas) to distract him with tales of (can you guess?) Afghanistan.

One would, I think, hardly have cared to be one of Doctor Watson's patients. He was so seldom there. However, there was at first some pretence of being concerned with medicine and he purchased 'a connection in the Paddington District' from 'old Mr Farquhar'. The tottering practice (old Mr Farquhar suffered from a species of St Vitus' Dance) had three advantages: it was better than the practice next door (Holmes observed that the step was worn three inches lower), there was a convenient substitute at hand, and it was near a station where 'railway cases were seldom trivial'. For the first three months he worked hard but the wretched man's heart was never in it

('My practice is never very absorbing') and after that it was simply fits and starts, cases 'of great gravity' and 'pressing professional business' alternating with absences of days at a time. How listless the bedside manner must have been. Sometimes even Holmes points out the path of duty: 'You want to go home, no doubt, Doctor?' 'Yes, it would be as well', but of course he is shortly back, armed, in Baker Street, and sipping from the spirit case and gasogene until all hours. A Kensington practice follows, from which he is secretly bought out by Holmes, and after that there is no more pretence, though he does sometimes take down a volume from his 'small medical shelf' and is always ready, should Holmes require it, with a diagnosis. Nor does his hand lose its cunning: asked by Holmes why Professor Presbury should move so mysteriously and on all fours down dark passages, Watson is not for a moment at a loss: 'Lumbago', he replies. It is not one of Holmes' tetchy days: 'We can hardly accept lumbago' is the only admonishment.

So it is back to Baker Street, in glorious permanence, with the fog swirling outside and cold partridge and Montrachet for supper, and the test tubes and the hydrochloric acid and the newly framed picture of General Gordon to feast the eyes on, and the visits to the Turkish Bath where Holmes is 'less reticent and more human than anywhere else' and cases can be discussed 'over a smoke in the pleasant lassitude of the drying-room'. And there are the occasional visits to Holmes' brother, Mycroft, and the sight of the 'beshawled and bediamonded' ladies outside the Lyceum. And there is the agreeable flutter of Holmes being offered a knighthood in 1902, and the solid comfort of knowing that one is John H. Watson, M.D. (why did his wife call him James?), late Indian Army, who played Rugger for Blackheath and was once thrown into the crowd at the Old Deer Park by 'Big Bob Ferguson'.

There are, to be sure, occasional clouds. When in teasing mood, Holmes can reply to an over-simple deduction by the Doctor with 'Excellent, Watson! You scintillate to-day'. But the mood was not always so. Even though he is feigning delirium (in *The Dying Detective*), Holmes comes out with some unpleasant truths: 'Facts are facts, Watson, and after all you are only a general practitioner with very limited experience and mediocre qualifications'. It does not need the Doctor to tell us that he is 'bitterly hurt'.

But he has his reward at last. He finds that he is more than the useful errand-boy, the bottle-washer, the willing horse. He is wounded in a shooting affray and Holmes, thinking the wound more serious than it is, allows something to pierce the bleak façade:

'You're not hurt, Watson? For God's sake, say that you
are not hurt'

My friend's wiry arms were round me and he was leading me to a chair.

'You're not hurt, Watson? For God's sake, say that you are not hurt.'

It was worth a wound — it was worth many wounds — to know the depth of loyalty and love which lay behind that cold mask. The clear, hard eyes were dimmed for a moment, and the firm lips were shaking. For the one and only time I caught a glimpse of a great heart as well as of a great brain. All my years of humble but single-minded service culminated in that moment of revelation.

Exactly. And what chance had poor Miss Mary Morstan against a moment such as that?

ADVICE FOR OPERATIC HEROINES

ADVICE FOR OPERATIC HEROINES

How one's heart bleeds for the tortured heroines of Grand Opera. We who plod Life's Highway have also our little personal tragedies and troubles, but theirs seem so immeasurably more complicated and unsettling. I do not, of course, refer to the fact that, Come Rain, Come Shine, they have to keep on singing. That is, as it were, part of the price: vocal expression of joy or woe is the very nature of the affair. But one would be stony-hearted indeed to feel no pang of pity as the great, crazed creatures come lumbering down-stage to pour into our eardrums generous lungfuls of their agitations. When Tosca climbs the battlements and peers nervously down into the abyss where she must shortly hurl herself, one wonders, in one's kindly way, whether there was not something, some helpful phrase, a few mumbled words of wise counsel which, tactfully whispered during Act I, would have made just all the difference.

But stay! There is still time. Before winter and the opera seasons are in full swing: before the *coulisses* of both hemispheres start ringing with garglings and spittings and foreign voices raised in furious altercation: before the chandeliers rattle and the *loges* bristle with lorgnettes: before the musicians scrape and blow and thud their way through Prelude and Intermezzo, let us attempt to sort out the problems of some of the more miserable song-birds. Let us straighten out their tangled lives as best we may and, as none of them appears very powerful intellectually, let us give our advice in the easily assimilated and genial form currently popular in our cheap (I speak financially) Ladies' Magazines:

Mimi (Paris) — You are young, dear, and Bohemians can, of course, be fascinating, but the *quartier* you inhabit sounds altogether too *artistique*. Can you not move to more wholesome surroundings (I understand that St. Cloud is delightful) and sew your seams there? Your painter friends seem, I admit, a very cheery crowd but don't besot yourself with this Rudolf. If he truly loves you he will come to visit you wherever you are, and if he does not — well there are plenty of other *poissons* in the *mer*, *n'est-ce pas*? Do do something about that cough; it may only be a tickle at present but just look what happened to Violetta! Luxivox Voice Pastilles are the very thing for your ailment: deliciously flavoured, they bring instant balm to — but you can read all about them on the tin.

Isolde (Cornwall) — It was a thousand pities that you ever left Ireland, and you were indeed unfortunate to have a maid who mixed the wrong drinks. I assume that the poison was in the usual dark-green bottle, and the love philtre in a container of some brighter hue. Is her eyesight poor, or (more likely, I fear) was she being deliberately perverse? One cannot trust servants to get a thing right these days, can one? I should, if I were you (and many of your sex would like to be), dally awhile with your two beaux and test the pair of them out. Break no hearts, mind, but allow yourself a year or two of thrilling indecision: a boating-picnic with one, a jousting-party with the other — but you know the sort of thing. You have certainly selected a lovely part of the world for it. Bodmin must be looking heavenly. Does Tristan fish?

Cio-Cio-San (Nagasaki) — He is only fooling with you, dear. Men are all the same, and sailors even more so. You are not in the sterling area, so stop singing (pretty, I grant, but where has it got you?) and go straight to the American Consul. He is sure to have a form for this kind of mishap. Tell him about the child, but better leave the little chap at home; two can be such a trying age and we don't want to spoil our trump card, do we? Then, to make quite sure, be at the quayside when your 'hubby's' ship docks. On this occasion, take Baby with you (Suzuki may care to stretch her legs at the same time). This cannot fail to bring you the helpful nest-egg that is yours by rights. How jolly that it will be in dollars: this is quite the pleasantest type of money to have nowadays.

Elsa (Antwerp) — I hardly know what to say, dear. I fully believe you when you say that your gentleman friend came By

Swan (a dear chum of mine, Senta, had a Dutch admirer who came By Phantom Ship), but I feel that I could advise you better if you would send me a 'snap' of your Mr Right. Meanwhile, do not press him for his name: let him be Schmidt or Robinsohn until he cares to tell you All. He will respect your trust. I am so glad that he has such a fine tenor voice: let Music, for the time being anyway, be your Bond. Are you really planning to settle in Holland? How fond are you of bulbs?

Don José (Seville) — You do not really belong on my page but your case has moved me. Leave this girl *at once*. Yes, I dare say she is very pretty and attractive and you may well be 'dotty' about her, but a chance meeting outside a cigarette factory is no proper commencement for a Life Partnership. It is not a good sign that she 'rows' with the other girls. The present price of cigarettes is, of course, her strong suit, but do not be blinded by an occasional smuggled 'fag'. Break away from Princess Nicotine, and from your own Princess at the same time. As you are in the Army, can you not apply for a compassionate posting to Barcelona? Go to the Adjutant and explain everything. He may then put the Welfare Officer on Carmen's tracks and get her into a really good Girls' Club. Oh dear, you are in a pickle, are you not?

Brünnhilde (Valhalla) — Yours, though worrying, seems to be largely a transportation problem and of course it is galling for a girl of your spirit to be seen constantly lugging dead heroes about. Can you not catch Wotan in a good mood and point out that you and your steed (Grani is it not?) are by no means as young as you were? Don't try to pull the wool over your father's eye as regards your age. Possibly, his sight being what it is, he has not noticed your exhaustion and you are to him still the 'girlie' of your early years. I do congratulate you, however, on keeping so cheerful at your work: 'Sing As You Go' is a grand motto. Now, settle down quietly somewhere (why not Shropshire?) and, if you feel that you don't want to get rusty, enter for an occasional point-to-point. I don't think that I should sing during any competitive riding: the other horses will not be accustomed to it and we don't want black looks in the unsaddling enclosure, do we? Do let me know when you are racing: I would love to venture a 'bob' or two. Good luck, dear, and keep those chins up.

MORE
SUNDAY BEST

REGAL REMNANTS

For some time now, kind and thoughtful and generous people who like, at birthdays and Christmas, to give a friend that Present That Is Different have kept a sharp look-out for announcements of those sales at which yet another 'fully authenticated' pair of Queen Victoria's knickers is due to come under the hammer.

The treasured garments are said to be constructed of a good durable linen, to be of extremely generous cut rather than fashionably form-hugging, and to be offered to the public at regular intervals, the last pair having been knocked down at auction for £284. Whether, after Albert's death, she went into black-bordered knickers I am unable to say but it seems a likely enough gesture in somebody who never did things by halves.

Although to talk of anything belonging to Queen Victoria as being 'knocked down' seems to savour of lèse-majesté, the supremely practical lady herself would surely have seen the point of the whole undertaking and would have commended it. 'We are glad that portions of our wardrobe are still of service and the price that they now appear to fetch is *most* gratifying.'

Of what the 'authentication' consists, who can say? The letters V.R. in a bold chain-stitch? A Cash's name-tape with 'Her Maj.' on it? Although a warning only to hand-wash them in a tepid Daz would be an anachronism, there may well have been some Buckingham Palace injunction of a similar nature and aimed at preventing a disastrous shrinkage. How many pairs, one idly wonders, are still in, so to speak, circulation? How many pairs were available for the royal needs at any one time? Hers was hardly a world of 'one on, one off, and one in the wash'.

Another clothing item from yesteryear, and a considerably older one, has recently and literally surfaced in the form of a Viking Warrior's woollen sock, not, one would have thought, even in its prime the most outstandingly fragrant of objects. It surged up from the depths of an Ouse bog which had preserved it, causing startled gasps among the members of a Viking archaeological dig and it is to receive a warm welcome ('This is an exciting find') in the Yorkshire museum for which it is destined and where, fully cleaned and freshened, and, possibly, delicately perfumed (you can't beat lavender), it will eventually be on view. Though normally a bit of a hothead, I find that I can, in this case, control my eagerness.

What other interesting articles may suddenly appear? I occasionally visit hospitable friends in Norfolk and in future and when in the Wash area I shall keep my eyes peeled for King John's carrier-bag, proudly labelled with what was the 1215 equivalent of Harrods or Sainsbury's and stuffed with the more portable of the crown jewels. Or further along the coast, and I seem to see it happening at Cromer, the discovery of a sea-soaked pair of sandals in a dark tan mock-leatherette would show plainly that Canute Was Here.

The distinguished historian, Hester Chapman, diligently researching into the early A.D. years, was finally able to state categorically that Queen Boadicea is buried beneath platform eleven at St Pancras. Here is a chance for British Rail to show what they are made of, as if we didn't know already. During one of the periods when trains are not, for some reason, running, why not dig up the platform and let us all have a thrilling dekko? Revered as she was, she is bound to have been laid to rest with various of her cherished 'personal things' — a bone comb, a chemise in mauve winceyette, a richly bejewelled stomacher, and even a pair of Y-fronts belonging to him whom the less austere Press would doubtless refer to as Husband Prasutagus.

Ought we not, for posterity's sake, each to prepare and bury our own Time Capsule, if that is the name, containing evidence of a representative day in one's merry life in this joyous year? I've got my artefacts all ready — some Typhoo tea-bags, a carton of All-Bran, a receipt for the water rates, a laundry bag of 'soil', an unfinished *Times* crossword and a disagreeably huffy letter from the Income Tax.

BOTTICELLIS AT BLETCHLEY

The cheering news that British Rail has nobly started to liberate for public viewing some of its works of art (purchased, and presumably as a speculation, by the British Rail Superannuation Fund) has set commuters' pulses racing up and down the country, for surely there is scope here for a pleasing travel amenity, to which I shall come in a moment.

The tasteful item now made visible by British Rail and at the National Gallery is a Chardin *Still-life with a dish of oysters and a bottle*, and a very fine example of simple realism it is too: you can reach out and almost *touch* those oysters or, better still, the bottle.

The works of art — furniture, pictures, sculptures — cover a wide range and those of us who have been worrying ourselves silly about the whereabouts of Tiepolo's *The Miraculous Translation of the Holy House of Loreto* will rejoice to know that it too is the property of wily British Rail, was recently on view, and is now snugly housed somewhere.

Ah, but where? What corner of the capital is considered safe for that Titian, those exquisite Bellinis, the T'ang and Ming vases and that famous Guardi (say him GOO-ARE-DEE). Are they perhaps under lock and key in the Goods Depot at Euston or the Paddington Left Luggage? Wiser never to reveal one's hiding-place, I suppose, in case some rascal should dart in and pinch one's Botticelli.

But now for my delightful plan. One hopes that the Chardin still-life is but a beginning and I have written to British Rail to suggest that their artistic treasures be regularly displayed — and the guard's van seems to be the absolutely ideal spot — as a visual treat and on all trains, however humble.

Thrilling indeed it would be to hear coming over the station loudspeakers enticing announcements such as 'The 10.15 for Watford will depart from Platform 3 and we have for you today

75

Spotti's superb *Femme Joyeuse*, together with, for furniture buffs, a very early Chippendale commode'.

Commuters eagerly walking to Egham Station for the 8.41 can tell from the ticket-collector's expression that something good is in store — his smile and those eyes merrily a-twinkle tell their own tale. 'How does Manet grab you?' he cries, absent-mindedly punching your season. 'Today you've got his original sketch for *Déjeuner sur l'Herbe* and quite a little bit of all right too. A little gem, frankly. Note the sensitive brushwork.'

Those rather grand trains . . . would run just as well and rapidly if called The Impressionist and The Picasso

British Rail will want, naturally, to cater for all tastes and the larger and lumpier Barbara Hepworths will be quite happy in that corner by the bicycles, with the guard keeping a watchful eye on them, not, heaven knows, to stop them getting stolen (their very weight rules out such a possibility) but to prevent angry people, as has been known, attacking them with their umbrellas.

As the idea catches on and enthusiasm grows, additional areas of the train can be used, with display cabinets gracing the walls of the buffet (say it BUFFY) and those munching an 'individual' pork pie and clutching a plastikup of warmish Speedikoff can at the same time feast their eyes on a Meissen figurine or a Derby dessert service. Then along to the guard's van they hurry for another admiring look at that unique quattrocento altar-piece.

Quite soon we shall find travellers choosing their trains by what they hope to find on them: 'I *always* catch the 9.40. Last week we had both a Rembrandt and a rather amusing little Marie Laurencin — yes, I know she's a lightweight but who cares?' And surely those rather grand trains that have got names (The Clansman, The Golden Hind) would run just as well and rapidly if called The Impressionist and The Picasso.

Well, there we are then. I myself shall be on the 10.30 for Exeter (some rather interesting Ch-ing jade last month). Let's meet in the buffy.

HO HO!

Those kind readers who have perhaps pictured me permanently tucked away in the west and put out to pasture in Devon's lush meadows will be astounded to learn that I have recently been in communication with the Mysterious East. Let me hasten to say that the communication was not telepathic but postal and I can tell you that it's been a real excitement to one who has only very seldom ventured further east than Margate.

Perhaps a more accurate description would be the Mysterious Middle East. Bulgaria in fact was where the letter came from, sent to my publishers and deftly forwarded on to me. Bulgaria must be, I think, part of the Balkans, that region whose agitations and political unrest and assassinations so often featured in the newspaper headlines of yesteryear as 'Trouble in the Balkans'.

My first thought was, naturally, that there was Trouble again and that my help was being enlisted as, possibly, an under-cover agent or some such. Fortunately a close study of Smiley's people (and oh my goodness, *how* they didn't smile!) has made me fully familiar with just what to do. I assume a gloomy expression, walk down a drab street and knock at a dingy door. A slatternly woman appears. I speak. 'I am Franz. I have come to see Olga. Are you Olga?' She looks shifty and replies, 'No, I am not Olga. Why you think I am Olga? I am Natalie. How could Natalie be Olga? Go away.' I then walk slowly off looking *pensif*, the better to muddle everybody. Gripping stuff, eh what?

Or perhaps, with thoughts again of yesteryear and that enjoyable game of warring armies, 'L'attaque', I might be an out-and-out spy, and the painted cardboard replica of 'L'espion' shows me just what to do and wear — dark blue two-piece serge suit and a black and broad-brimmed Homburg hat in which to peer out suspiciously and from behind a tree at

78

troop movements, behaviour guaranteed to cause instant arrest and execution. It never seemed odd, sixty or so years ago and with the Great War only just over, that the 'L'attaque' opposing forces should be represented as being French and English. Old habits die hard.

However, the letter, very handsomely stamped and whizzed to me at lightning speed by the European P.O.s (such an example to others), turned out to be from the House of Humour and Satire at Gabrovo and it said, by way of explanation, that the House's object in life was the POPULARIZING OF HUMOUR OF THE PEOPLES. Fun, in fact, was the purpose of the enterprise, and what could be jollier?

The letter invited me, in charmingly phrased sentences, to take part in various creative activities, all aimed at making the peoples go Ho Ho and cause the entire Balkans to ring with merry chuckles. To get in the swim, I could either do a satirical picture of my own designing or paint a portrait of an 'outstanding humorist' and so, for starters, I'm aiming at a gouache of Mr Benn which may well win me the Committee of Culture's Prize of 1,000 *leva* (plural of *lev* and about £633, but of course it's the kudos I'm really after).

Or there is sculpture, which has to be three-dimensional (surely easier than two) and in 'durable material', which rather rules out my plasticine Eros, in addition to the fact that though one has sometimes suspected sculptors of having us all on (a lady with no stomach and nine breasts and called Eve Triumphant), it is not easy to get a satirical or otherwise laugh out of inanimate lumps of this and that.

But cheer up for there is one field of humour and satire that seems to offer endless possibilities for everybody and I refer to 'Laughter Photos'. These are happy snaps 'which point to the funny side of life' (first prize, gold plaque and a 20-day holiday in Bulgaria). Here I am going to go all out and am entering (a) my Devon grandmother rigged up for Matins on a cold day, (b) the Oundle School staff of 1899, (c) the widowed Queen Victoria gazing grumpily at a bust of Albert, and (d) a close-up of the wicket-keeper achieving a stumping during a needle girls' cricket match at Roedean. That plaque is as good as mine.

OUCH!

Two interesting items of scholastic news that have recently made the headlines, and to which I shall later return, have prompted me to add a third, though perhaps the fact is already known to many that the schoolmaster Alfred Pocock, great-uncle of the celebrated cricketer, W. G. Grace, invented a caning machine for use on idle or insubordinate pupils.

Did he, one so wonders, patent it? Are there somewhere in some dusty Record Office full details and diagrams of the ingenious contraption, with pulleys here and ropes there and birch twigs everywhere? The year of this punitive breakthrough was about 1835 and so was the machine steam-driven or was reliance placed on stout elastic bands? Wind power would have been too chancy for, with the victim strapped down and at the ready, one could hardly hang about and wait for a strong north-caster.

There was, presumably, a dial that could be set to administer the required number of whacks — just the round dozen, say — and this seems to me to answer at least half of the objections lately raised by The Society of Teachers Opposed to Physical Punishment (STOPP for short) which complains, I gather, about the 'indignity' of corporal punishment both to the giver and to the taker. For now, with the latter firmly clamped into position (see fig 14) and Pocock's Patent all set to give of its best, the schoolmaster can beat a dignified retreat to his study and, if he is in Holy Orders, con over his notes for his next sermon on the text 'He giveth his cheek to him that smiteth him'. Those masters with abnormally keen hearing may care to pop in a pair of ear-plugs until Pocock clicks to a standstill.

STOPP has also, it seems, got it in for the providers of advertisements of the Bognor Cane Company, which sells 'spanking paddles' at, I am told, a very reasonable figure and with, I dare say, a reduction for quantity. In my day, both as canee and caner (though not very much of either), the instruments used were known in the trade as Young Gentlemen's Correction Switches, but *plus ça change* and all that . . .

However, the members of STOPP, so mindful of the tender susceptibilities both of their colleagues and of the youthful charges in their care, can cheer up no end by perusing a 64-page book called *English for Life* and intended to assist school leavers with but limited achievements to their credit and about to launch themselves onto the world.

From the newspaper account of the book in question, it all seems most helpful — instruction as to how to write letters, how to answer the telephone in an acceptable manner, how to collate statistics, how to make lists of things — and it is only when we come to the advice on Interviews that one gets a little uneasy. There is a reference to your 'prospective employer', which seems to me to be the wrong way round and to set the tone for what follows.

For among the questions which the prospective employee is encouraged to ask are those referring to tea breaks (can there be a section called How Not To Make A Bad Impression?), luncheon vouchers, holidays, overtime, bonuses, hours of work and, oh dear me, unions. From there it seems to me to be only a step to the employee asking to be shown, at the factory gates, where the picket line forms up and how to get the best volume of sound out of the melodious word SCAB.

Against this barrage of self-centred questions, the employer is, I suppose, expected to remain respectfully silent, apart from supplying such answers as he may be able to give, and I see now that, when as a prospective schoolmaster I went for an interview with the one who was to be my future headmaster, I did all the wrong things. I didn't, in fact, ask a single question. I just answered them.

Bachelor public schoolmasters now, I am informed, get very fussed about what their accommodation will be. How *many* sitting-rooms? Is there a pantry as well as a kitchen? Is there a second bathroom in case one has somebody to stay? In my case it turned out to be a shared bathroom and available for my use for half an hour three times a week. If I lingered a single second over the half hour I would have found myself in the bath with Matron ('after you with the Camay').

DON'T PUT THAT IN YOUR PIPE

Although Miss Irene Dunne tunefully informed us in an early-ish talking picture (wasn't it *Roberta*, and in about 1935?) that smoke gets in your eyes, a fact already known to many who had either puffed or were puffed at, we have since, and quite rightly, been cautioned that cigarette smoke gets into much more damaging places and one can but applaud BBC1 and Dr Miriam Stoppard, both of them helping fragrant-weed-users to kick, as we 'with it' people phrase it, the habit.

One does rather wonder what kind of reception an anti-smoking campaign would have got fifty or sixty years ago. A fairly chilly one, I should imagine, for social life, literature and the theatre all relied heavily upon tobacco. In 1924 the curtain of Mr Coward's play, *The Vortex*, had not been up fifteen seconds before Helen, 'smartly dressed and thirty', asked for a cigarette, while the stage directions for the week-end party in Act II contain the line 'the air is black with cigarette smoke and superlatives'.

As Dolores, the dusky charmer in the musical play, *A Southern Maid*, José Collins sang the famous 'Cigarette' song ('It's a pleasure divine when your lip is on mine'), subsequently hurling the smoking object from her with a gesture of which ASH would have warmly approved, the butt being carefully collected by a stage-hand and given to admiring Collins fans (they called themselves the KOJs — Keen On José) at the stage-door.

The entire plot of *Dangerous Corner* (1932) depends upon a musical cigarette box. In all of Gerald du Maurier's plays, one of the treats of the evening was to see the nonchalance with which he lit up. If, in those far-off days, Richard Rodgers' hills had been alive, they would not have been alive with the sound of music but with the sound of coughing.

One of the most important poems of the great middle years

of Miss Ella Wheeler Wilcox begins with the line 'I was smoking a cigarette', a line which would now, I suppose, have to be changed to 'Despite a government health warning, I was smoking a cigarette'. In novels, heroines were apt to loll about in hammocks musing about Life and 'lazily' blowing smoke rings, by no means an easy achievement. Previous to this, a rejected suitor had sometimes 'angrily' stubbed out ('Is that your final answer, Monica?') a Balkan Sobranie.

Some brute has pinched my only copy and so I cannot verify the reference but wasn't it Bulldog Drummond whose cigarette-case sported two sorts ('Turkish this side, Virginian that')? Did Phyllis Benton, his wife-to-be, then select a Virgin, as they were racily called, and apply a Swan Vesta? How sadly one forgets these pleasing facts.

Despite head-shakings and mutterings that smoking 'stunted growth', everybody's first act in the prep school special train that whisked us from Hampshire to Waterloo and the hols was to light up a Woodbine. We were then about eleven years old and those who didn't immediately turn green and be sick felt tremendously sophisticated ('Another fag, anybody?').

A sort of blessing was conferred on smoking by some of those prominent in fiction and fact. Sherlock Holmes (fiction) encouraged poor muddled old Watson to smoke cigars and himself made great play with that curly meerschaum, while Baldwin (fact, alas) was inseparable from the pipe that seemed itself to breathe forth reliability and solidity and peace. Red Indians, also keen on peace, smoked in a very chummy manner, sharing both the communal pipe and, I rather fear, communal dribble.

Every theatre programme bore the acknowledgement 'Cigarettes by Abdulla'. Even Queen Mary was said to be a slave to nicotine, while ladies of title, fearful that their guilty secret would be discovered, smoked in their bedrooms, deceitfully exhaling up the chimney. Men wore special jackets for smoking in, and every sizeable house had a smoking-room. The fact that cigarettes were jocularly known as 'coffin-nails' deterred nobody.

Tobacco once supplied me, previously a heavy smoker but

long since reformed, with a merry moment. During the war, cigarettes were sometimes sold not in packets but in handfuls or multiples of five. Calling one day at a kiosk for a supply, the sad-faced *vendeuse* said to me, 'Sorry, dear, no Passing Clouds today. In fact, the only thing I can offer you is ten loose Churchmen'.

SING AS YOU GO

It always seemed to me, as a schoolmaster struggling away, and a good many years ago now, to teach French, that the things to try to avoid in the classroom were monotony and boredom and therefore my heart-felt admiration goes out to the spirited Staffordshire schoolmistress, Miss Frankman, who was recently reported in a newspaper as 'singing arias between lessons'.

What could be more stimulating than this very unusual scholastic treat? Just picture the excitement when, with the last algebraic equation successfully solved, the final isosceles trapezium drawn, the teacher clears her throat and inflates her lungs, the thrilling 'ping' of the tuning-fork is heard and then a great burst of Verdi rings out and rattles the blackboard. Miss Frankman is, it seems, a mezzo-soprano and therefore operates in that deliciously rich chest-note area that lies between soprano and alto, and very agreeable it must be to hear her at it. Would I were in her 'junior school'.

There is said to be nothing new under the sun but surely this inter-lesson warbling is a complete novelty. For a precedent, one searches, naturally, the schoolgirl stories of Miss Angela Brazil, and I may tell you that one searches in vain. It is true that in *Jean's Golden Term* there is a good deal of singing and instrumental playing, with Vera Anderson on violin, Sheila Pritchard on piano and Jean herself on guitar ('I got those wretched crotchets and quavers mixed') but their headmistress, Miss Suffolk, though gifted in other ways, attempts no operatic arias.

And in *At School With Rachel* the heroine muffs things badly in the cantata ('Rachel bungled her top notes') but the music mistress, a Miss Hampton, sets no vocal example and totally fails to give musical tongue herself. So I think we can safely assume that the excellent Miss Frankman has broken entirely new ground.

One only hopes that the pleasing innovation will catch on and will be very widely imitated in both girls' and boys' schools. We all know what Music While You Work did for the war effort (snatches from Eric Coates were said to accelerate the production line like billy-o) though here it would be more in the nature of Music Before And After You Work and a potent incentive to master those irregular verbs or that chemical formula: and then hooray for some Donizetti!

School notice-boards could usually do with a little cheering up for they normally only show details of rugger or net-ball teams ('The following will play against Dumbleton on Upper Sixpenny . . .') or cryptic announcements of, to an outsider, a somewhat sinister sort: 'Philbrick, Measures and Masterton are to go to Miss Battersby at 4 p.m.' So why not enliven matters by providing the day's musical programme?

- 'Mr Wheatcroft (Classical Remove). 11 a.m. 'On With The Motley' and if time allows, 'Your Tiny Hand Is Frozen, Let Me Warm It Into Life'.
- 'Miss Willard (IV B). 12.15 p.m. 'Come Then, Dearest, Here I'm Waiting, Wildly Panting Is My Heart' from *La Giaconda*. Miss Willard will give an encore ('Companion Gay, Go Not Away') after Fire Drill.
- 'Mr Stirling-Jones (Shell) regrets that he has laryngitis but hopes, as soon as he is fit, to continue with Gems from *Parsifal*.'

Headmistresses, interviewing prospective biology teachers ('What experience have you of newts?') and reading their testimonials ('She has been a cheery presence in the lab') will also require to know their operatic range and preferences ('I'm afraid that our good Miss Harrison has already rather ''cornered'' *Aida*'). Headmasters, sifting through the answers to an advertisement for 'Good post for somebody offering woodwork and divinity in progressive school. Salary . . .', will thrust aside the 'Said to be good mixer' replies and will pounce on 'Music-lover with pleasing tenor voice'.

Oh to be young again, for a joyous and tuneful future awaits schoolchildren. The corridors will resound with *Rigoletto*. There will be *Faust* at lunch and a bartered bride in the boot-room and not only the hills will be alive with the sound of music.

SITTING ON A FORTUNE

When uttered in the bosom of the family, the phrase 'I've got a new club' can mean different things. A good few years ago, when home was on the open plan system and consisted of a roomy cave ('Do wipe your boots, Odo dear, I've just put fresh rushes down'), the club would be likely to have iron spikes let into it and would be vigorously used for acquiring food and property and womenfolk and other desirables not belonging at that time to the club's wielder. And in this connection it would be linguistically incorrect to refer to his victims as being club-bable chaps.

Nearer our times and in Wentworth and Sunningdale circles, the new club could only mean a gleaming No. 3 iron or, in the era when golf implements were allowed to have pleasantly individual names, a cleek or a brassie or a mashie-niblick. In those dear old days, golf buffs tended to call their houses 'Pin High' or 'Dormy Two' or even 'Rub-O'-The-Green' and their conversation mainly recalled moments of high personal drama on the links ('I was one up at the turn and then suddenly started to shank').

But nowadays, alas, the words 'new club' only very rarely mean the opening of one of those establishments which are often in the St James's area of London and which house — and here one flies to splendid old Chambers, such a pal when one is at a verbal loss — 'an association of persons who possess a building as a common resort for the members'. For clubs do not increase in number. They either amalgamate to keep alive or, if no presentable bedfellows present themselves, close their doors.

The Bath Club, where youthful royalty learnt ('Kick *harder*, your royal highness') to trudgen, has disappeared and others of an equal standing have already passed into oblivion. Some have attempted to inject new life in various ways, and a very famous club, The Reform, has decided to admit women members, and this unisex fashion may well spread. Clubs, like so many other things, are no longer what they once were.

Or are they? In the club to which I am happy to belong, there is no feeling of panic. Members, sinking down after lunch ('Did you have the saddle, Jasper? It was first rate') into the leather armchairs in which they plan to spend the afternoon, seem to have no fear of the bailiffs, or of whoever would come rudely in to disintegrate a bankrupt club. The air is filled with gentle sighs which give way to rhythmic breathing and then to snores. The traffic rumbling past in Pall Mall is not alone in providing rumbles. All is peace and in an hour or so the distant tinkling of tea-cups tells of the approach of further creature comforts. There is nothing like the thought of a toasted tea-cake dribbling butter for stopping snorers snoring and returning them to active life.

An idea, financially quite promising and inspired by indispensable Chambers, has come to me. It was the words 'persons who possess a building' that sparked it off. Who but the present members can possibly be said to own a club and its contents? And, if a club has to close, who but the present members should share the rich rewards of selling its furnishings ('What am I offered for these 849 yards of Turkey carpeting?') and the doubtless immensely valuable land on which it stands? Not even lawyers, trained to eschew the obvious and to go against anything that sounds like being common sense, could find anything wrong with this reasoning.

And so here's my plan. No club that is on the skids is going to be too choosey about the new members that it enrols and it might be well worth while, as a spec, to scout about a bit and hastily join all those clubs that seem to be on the way out. I personally shall set to work at once and, in cases where the club-houses are of little or no architectural interest, I may even try to hurry matters along a little. I wonder if that bulldozer fellow, who got into a muddle and razed to the ground an ancient building that was listed as not to be razed, is doing anything in the next fortnight.

TEA FOR TWO

Egon Ronay would seem to have at least two claims to fame, his constantly reiterated lack of pleasure, to put it mildly, in certain public eating places, and the fact that his name must surely have been the inspiration behind Beachcomber's famous character, Egon Toast.

Mr Ronay certainly has on toast those gilded palaces of gourmet joy, motorway cafés, but how jolly to find him saying a word of warm appreciation of, in the quiet streets of country towns, old-fashioned tea-rooms 'run by perfectionist ladies or married couples dedicated to sheer hard work allied to skill and producing unsurpassed excellence'.

Well said indeed, and immediately one sees in the grateful mind's eye an endless line of such establishments visited in the past — the bow window with its crisply laundered net curtains and discreet list of prices, and the door that, when opened, gives that loud pinging sound to alert Deborah and Deirdre, hovering expectantly, to the welcome arrival in their midst of Trade. On the counter, beside the tastefully arranged vase of wild grasses and poppies ('Oh, that's Deirdre's department'), is an assortment of delicious home-made fudge, seldom underpriced.

The besmocked Deborah takes your order ('We do an Inclusive Tea at 90p') and in due course there arrives on your circular oaken table a real feast — fresh scones and farmhouse butter and marrow jam (is there any better?), Earl Grey from a charming china tea-pot and drunk from pretty cups, and then a splendid choice of cakes, all of them constructed on the premises by an unseen toiler in the back regions ('Any more walnut loaf, Prue? And we could do with more ginger-snaps'). Deirdre collects your cash ('Let's see, you were the two Inclusives, were you not?') and you exit, fully replete and satisfied and with half a pound of fudge for luck.

Time was when tea-rooms were large and commercially more professional and it was considered impossible to be able to consume tea without the presence of potted palms and music, the latter being provided by a trio, usually feminine, of piano, violin and 'cello. Led by the violinist, pince-nez gleaming, they played selections from *Lilac Time* and *Our Miss Gibbs* while one pondered yet again on the many problems and difficulties confronting a lady 'cellist who wants to look her best, in addition to conveying her instrument from place to place. And here too

They played selections from *Lilac Time* and *Our Miss Gibbs*

there were usually to be found, not gracious china tea-pots and hot-water jugs, but those devilish shiny metal contraptions where the manufacturer's aim appears to have been to concentrate the main body of heat in the handle, and then sadistically enjoy the customer's screams of pain when trying to lift the thing up and swing it into infusive action.

People visiting London and requiring tea are nowadays in for a thin time. Gone are the ABCs. Gone are the Corner Houses and the lovely Lyon's tea-rooms. Gone are those attractive 'Nippy' waitresses, order pads at the ready and with an HB snatched from coils of hair somewhere behind their right ear. Gone is Gunter's, that provider, in Curzon Street, of the world's best gâteaux. Gone is the Carlton Hotel tea-lounge where Phyllis Benton first met Bulldog Drummond (the sinister Dr Lakington was, in Sapper's words, 'tea-ing' there too). And gone, alas, are those aptly-named Fullers and their mouth-watering chocolate layer cakes.

London clubs, in addition to supplying at lunch time such ancient treats as jam roly-poly and apple charlotte, also provide tea (toasted buns and slices of rich Dundee cake) but where else to turn? Readily available at all hours of the day, and for all I know of the night also, is what must be the world's least attractive culinary invention, the pizza. I also see, here and there, dark-brown chickens sullenly revolving in some oriental cooking apparatus. Not for me, thank you, or the greasy hamburgers and double order of chips ('After you with that ketchup').

Perhaps in the City, where so much good food is available, there still lurk a few proper tea-shops. Is there possibly some forgotten Lyon's? If I were ever to be lost, parched and starving, in the Sahara Desert, my own personal mirage would be a pot of tea, a plate of 'fancies' and a couple of jolly Nippies called Mona and Monica.

AFTER ALL

Splendid tales, some of them possibly apocryphal, used to be told of a delightfully eccentric Winchester schoolmaster who, reminiscing one day about the past, was heard to say 'The year my first wife died, I also lost my umbrella with the cherrywood handle'.

And indeed on being informed, in suitably dignified terms, by the doctor that the said wife, lying seriously ill upstairs, had finally kicked the bucket, he heaved a sigh and summed up the busy events of a schoolmaster's troubled day with 'It never rains but it pours'.

Doubtless he would have had something equally illuminating to say about the snow that has recently descended on Europe in, in some sad cases, such disastrously lavish quantities. The Badminton Library of sporting pastimes used to publish a volume which gave helpful advice about a safe method of negotiating deep snow and I recall an extremely alarming illustration of a man who had foolishly ignored their warnings about snowshoes and was to be seen buried up to his armpits and in grave danger of an icy death. And printed beneath the picture was SERVE HIM RIGHT!

Readers will be in no way surprised to learn that I have never taken part in winter sports. Quite frankly, my generous build and fully fleshed-out limbs aren't absolutely ideal for such activities though I can see my weight making a valuable contribution to a toboggan in its downward progress on the Cresta Run. But I really wouldn't be up to those things constantly brought to us on the telly — sensational jumps, that speedy wiggle-waggle through beflagged posts, and that breathtaking rush down what I think is known as the *piste*. One is only human and, provided that no necks are broken, it is only natural to sit up and take greater interest when one of the skiers comes a real purler and disappears in a whirling, swirling conglomeration of arms, legs, skis and snow.

But some years ago I was once, persuaded and invited by a kind and generous friend, in St Moritz at winter sports time and staying in an outstandingly elegant hotel where every other person looked either like a famous oil magnate or an exiled king: and indeed was. Ex-schoolmasters look like nothing so much as ex-schoolmasters and so one cut little ice, or needed to.

Watching the daytime activities such as skiing, jumping, skating and curling, I developed a wild urge to take part in some way and, spotting one morning some children sliding happily downhill on a wooden contraption which seemed to be called 'a luge', I confided in my friend a wish to join them and slide too. After a sharp intake of breath, he gave me an anxious look and said 'Well, it will have to be a huge luge', and so I abandoned the idea.

All this was at a time when the smart, weekly illustrated magazines still took a quite disproportionate interest in winter sports and upper-crust St Moritz visitors in particular. Glossy page after glossy page featured 'The Hon. Petronella Ailment, known to her wide circle of friends as "Potty", exchanging the latest *on dit* with Viscount Tweezer', and toothy smiles were to be seen on all sides as 'Lady Merrilyn Forceps ventures on to the *piste* with her youngest daughter, "Scrap"'. Occasionally an amusing mishap on the skating rink (Lord Tynte crashing into Miss 'Bumps' Crabtree and sending her flying) was presented with just the cheery sub-title, 'Ooooops!'

Tremendous emphasis was always laid on the obviously highly important happening known to everybody as *après ski*. I could never quite make out whether this referred to the clothes they all wore after skiing, or to the drinks they drank, the dinner they ate, the flirtations they flirted and the bedtime yawns they yawned. Wiser perhaps not to think of yawns in this connection.

Returning after all these exciting experiences and quite happily to my placid and unglossy life in Devon, I began to think of this *après* business, but attempts in winter to smarten myself up and to make popular among my friends the words *après*-Scrabble and, in summer, *après*-croquet sadly failed.

TRY IT ON

Before passing on to less agitating matters, and in view of the enormous number of letters I have received, all supportive save one (and she a French woman), pray allow me a final squeak of dismay about the appalling Chunnel, clearly wanted and needed by virtually nobody (well, ask around among your friends). And furthermore, I have an important question to put.

Whose idea was it to give a sort of spurious holy aura, the blessing of the Church as it were, to the signing of the Agreement by staging it in the Chapter House of Canterbury Cathedral, in the county much of whose beauty is to be ruined? The French, far stricter in religious matters, offered us no cathedral when we went over there to sign and just made do with the Lille Town Hall, and perfectly adequate it was too. Incidentally, our signing took place on Ash Wednesday, whatever that may indicate (I cannot think that ashes rank very high on the Good Omen List).

For the frivolous there was, however, one pleasing moment, for when the telly showed the two chief participants signing and then, wildly smiling, exchanging those red leather folders, handsomely tooled no doubt, the scene looked exactly like the opening of an episode of 'This Is Your Life' and one hoped that M. Mitterand was going to turn out to be Eamonn Andrews in disguise, genially embarking on the well known ritual — 'You were born Margaret Hilda Roberts in Grantham and here is an early snap of you as a kiddie in Dad's grocery store peeping shyly round the bacon counter'. And on to the closing moment when an aged relative aged ninety-seven is specially flown from Tasmania ('Hello, Mag! Long time no see!').

And now, as prolonged disapprobation of both Prime Ministers and tunnels has never really been my line, allow me to be sunny side up once more and hurry forward with an excellent piece of advice, advice that is rather different from that supplied recently by a friend who, promising that it is true, assures me that he was somewhat startled a few months ago by hearing his letter-box flap clatter and, hastening into the hall, finding in the box a printed card which just said WHY NOT TAKE ADVANTAGE OF YOUR MILKMAN?

My advice concerns clothing. For those who didn't happen to see the American edition of the glossy magazine *Vogue* for October, 1985, let me hurriedly fill you in. A columnist, expatiating about the very tricky changes of temperature and climatic conditions in America, produced the memorable words, 'New York isn't easy. Bring a fur'. Readers of glossy magazines are doubtless themselves glossy and therefore possess furs and thus are going to be nice and snug on Madison and 54th, and so hooray for that, but what advice would one give in a magazine dealing with weather conditions in our own capital? 'London can be a difficulty. Bring macintosh, umbrella, galoshes, Balaclava, fur-lined gloves, Kosiglow *lingerie* (and kindly DON'T SAY IT, as so many now do, LON-GER-RAY) and just about half a ton of Kleenex tissues.'

But, good though that is, that isn't really my special bit of advice, which concerns bodily heat loss. I recall, about two years ago, a telly lecture aimed at the dim-witted section, of which I am a founder member. It explained vividly and pictorially and by means of goodness knows what scientific tricks how warmth escapes from the body and there, alarmingly, were shimmering heat rays flying in quite disastrous quantities out of the model's head. Up and away they went, to be lost for ever. You may have thought possibly the stomach or, pardon me, the buttocks were more closely concerned with heat loss and possible hypothermia. Apparently not.

And so I beg, and in cold snaps I beg ever more seriously, everybody of 'a certain age' (polite words for sixty plus) to wear indoors some sort of woolly hat or bonnet or head-covering. Warm as toast you'll be. If you haven't ever tried it, try it now. I really mean it. The results amaze one, and who cares what you look like?

Well, somebody does. I was urging this practice on a reluctant woman friend (reluctant to adopt it, I mean, rather than reluctant to be a friend), for ever complaining of the cold. 'I'm going to look very silly', she said, 'dusting with a hat on.' 'You'll look sillier still', I said, 'stone dead and dusting the pianola.'

BUT ONCE A YEAR

In early January, friendly Christmas cards continue to arrive, struggling gamely home like the last few straggling runners on a London Marathon — whiskery and obese old Santas merrily cramming their pot-bellies and bulging sacks down chimneys, olde worlde coachloads of crimson-cheeked revellers setting happily off at a spanking clip-clop through the snow, horns tooting, skaters gliding smoothly over a frozen Thames, and young men pouncing on startled girls ('Caught you') as they blush becomingly beneath the mistletoe.

My most un-Christmassy card so far has been a rather splendid The Tower of London At Dusk, a forbidding enough construction at the best of times and in bright sunlight. Not even the presence of a posse of jolly old beefeaters gathering in the gloom can make one forget the axe and the block and the heads falling. But kindly meant, no doubt, with its inspiriting accompanying verse:

> Even if the weather's drear,
> May your day be full of cheer.

Which of us, involved in the anticlimatic aftermath of Christmas and now at the period when the noble turkey is being diminished and minced into tasty croquettes (you just egg-and-breadcrumb them and fry until golden brown) and slices of unused plum pudding grace the table in a similarly fried condition (not the only thing, ha ha, that's been fried!), does not at some point suffer from a strong feeling of guilt?

Not, perhaps, at the volume of food consumed and booze boozed, for most of us have had to work hard for them, but at the memory of some friend forgotten, some gift unbought, some cheap and inadequate card sent in return for a large and handsome Houses of Parliament By Moonlight (or should it be Moonshine?) with an unerased '85p' on the back of it.

Bad too are the guilty feelings of those who have taken a firm line and, instead of buying cards, have generously sent money to Oxfam. And now they have to pay for the gesture and all over the country apologetic letters, usually written by the lady of the house, are on their way to their raised-eyebrow recipients ('I simply *cannot* think why we haven't heard from Hilda').

'Dearest Cynthia,
    Your saucy Cock Robin was by far our prettiest card and has taken pride of place on the mantelpiece next to Gerry's mother! Such a chirpy little person (the robin, I mean!!) who seems to be insisting that we go out at once and buy him yet another packet of SWOOP. *Where* did you find him, you clever creature?
    We're all in good trim here, apart from a few seasonal sniffles, and I know that you'll understand when I tell you that this year Gerry and I decided that, instead of cards . . .'

Then there are those warm-hearted people who like, in their own phrase, to 'keep up' with and send cards to chance acquaintances made many years ago. Letters are needed here too:

'Dear Mrs Whitten,
    That Loughborough post-mark told us to whom we owed the really beautiful reproduction of Clotti's oil of "Christmas Roses" even before we spotted your "Cheerio from The Whittens" inside! Bless you both for always remembering us so nicely. How time flies, and that heavenly fortnight at that Scarborough hotel seems like yesterday instead of 1962 (was it?).
    We often talk of you both and your darling old Scottie, Mac — such a courageous and lively old chap for 17, and of course we chuckle anew over his various 'escapades' and watery misdeeds (pardon my French, as Mr W would say!). How fortunate it was that the hotel proprietor was such a doggy person too. I do hope that one day we may "coincide" there again. Have you another Scottie? A friendly pat from us both, if so.
    As it happens, this year — and it was my husband's idea — we decided . . .'

ON TOAST

Those of us who, in the early-morning and sometimes wakeful hours of the night, start to worry about this and that, anxieties which frequently include fretful thoughts about life beyond the Iron Curtain and their Plans for the Future, can now worry a good bit less for over there they have found something to distract their minds from nuclear matters. A reliable daily paper informs us that the Russians have, at long last, discovered toast.

Many of us have from childhood on been taking toast for granted and happily wielding wire toasting-forks in front of glowing coal fires, adjusting the length of the fork as heat and occasion demand. We have therefore grown accustomed to the beauties of toast — its smell, its colour, its texture and, when spread with butter and lightly sprinkled with salt, its (to borrow an advertising term) crunchy goodness.

Not so the Russians, poor things, with their porcelain stoves and absence of open fires and, therefore, toasting forks. There is certainly no mention of toast in *War and Peace*. Hunt as one may through the packed pages of *Das Kapital*, ever one's favourite reading and, in translation, presumably a required book for all Russians, you will find that Karl Marx skips toast, and this despite the fact that for quite a time he was resident in England at 28, Dean Street, Soho, where the eye-opening availabilities must surely have included toast. Nobody in the plays of Chekhov rings the bell and demands, from one of those depressed and decrepit old servants, a rackful of toast.

But now, we are told, electric toasters are becoming all the rage and are flying off the assembly lines, while a wild, nay almost unbridled, enthusiasm for toast sweeps the Steppes. Furthermore, a Soviet weekly magazine points out, in a thoughtful article, the advantageous fact that stale bread makes, within reason, excellent toast, often better than fresh bread,

101

and thus and hey-presto, every old scrap of bread in the bin can
be used up. Spread it with butter or jam (the text seems to hint
that Lenin wouldn't have approved of people spreading with
both) and away down the red lane with it. 'Believe me, it's
tasty', the author of the article adds, though one hardly knows
what on earth that would come out as in Russian.

The thing to say is 'Apple Pudding'

Who can tell what toast might not have achieved in the way of making Stalin jollier? A few toasted chunks of best wholemeal thickly covered with Devon butter and then lightly dusted with the Russian equivalent of Gentleman's Relish, might have turned him into quite a fun person. Not easy, of course, for a novice to guide a sizeable *bouchée* of hot toast past those luxuriant Stalin moustachios and into the main working area, but who would have minded a lingering and whisker-held crumb or two or an outlying blob of butter or Relish, prior to their being retrieved with the tongue? And the result? Sunny Joe himself.

What other treasured British munchables might prove popular? Some are rather doubtful. At the end of the war I found myself in an Allied delegation to the German headquarters at Flensburg and, at mealtimes, seated next to a Russian officer. Attempts at chatty conversation ('Have you come far?' and 'How nice to see the sun again!') brought no response. Perhaps an aunt had died in Siberia. At breakfast the late enemy, possibly to curry favour, produced platefuls of porridge for us and the Russian, after some thought, seized a knife and spread the porridge liberally on a slice of bread, so perhaps they're not quite ready yet for porridge.

I seem to see Russians enjoying our nice old-fashioned English puddings such as Spotted Dick (the name could easily be changed to Spotted Igor), Tipsy Cake (slosh on the vodka), Treacle Tart, Jam Roly-Poly and Apple Pudding.

As to the last-named, let me pass on a tip. Some photographers when encouraging sitters to 'look pleasant please' suggest that they utter the word 'Cheese'. Quite wrong. A swiftly ejaculated 'Cheese' imparts to the face a forced and strained look. The thing to say is 'Apple Pudding', after which a pleasingly alert expression graces the features. If you prefer to say 'Summer Pudding' that's up to you but the result will be the same.

WILLINGLY TO SCHOOL

Middle-aged or elderly readers, still somewhat resentful of the less stimulating facets of their school days (algebra, Ohm's Law, dreadful Frog irregular verbs such as *ouïr*, and St Paul's endless journeys, enlivened by all too few shipwrecks) must now regret not having been born many years later.

Everything is easier these days and is going to be easier still, for an enlightened reformer has come up with a suggestion about the 'relevant use of spare time hobbies' that may well revolutionize our entire educational system.

This scholastic pioneer, a distinguished member of a university Research Department and bent on helping 'those who are not particularly interested in school', claims that fishing lessons (and apparently fly-fishing especially) have 'motivated' backward children to concentrate on other subjects and he calls boldly for a CSE fishing examination. It seems that one big London comprehensive has already seen the light and is successfully teaching fishing, while the provision of school trout hatcheries is under lively consideration by this splendidly go-ahead Department.

What could be better? Instead of those depressing and useless Latin sentences, such as 'Those who were in front fell on those who were behind' and 'Dig a ditch 12 feet wide', all is changed. Now, on entering the classroom, Mr Turnbull simply cries 'To the river!' and, clutching up rods and landing nets and one or two Blue Zulus (flies, I hasten to explain), away they all go.

I have to confess (and do please observe how 'with it' and racy my language has become) that I am not completely 'clued up' on trout, beyond knowing how to squeeze lemon over them in the stillness of death and then happily munch them, hot or cold, down.

I would therefore be a little apprehensive about tackling my O Level Fishing. Whatever would the questions be like?

(a) An expert has written, 'Avoid bulky flies'. Discuss.

(b) Answer two of the following: – Do trout smell? Can trout smell? Could sea-trout be persuaded that they are still at sea by shaking a generous measure of Cerebos into their tank?

Fishing is, presumably, to be a unisex activity and will pose problems in a girls' school for poor Miss Merridew, anxious to begin her stinks lesson and with her Bunsen already excitingly alight. 'Where is Prudence Willoughby?' she asks, to which the answer might be 'She's out collecting maggots' or 'I'm afraid that Prudence fell head first into the hatchery, Miss Merridew, and Matron is drying her things'.

But just picture the excitement of Prize Day, with a purple and obese Sir Somebody Something doing the honours: '. . . and finally, I will ask Blossom Faraday, who beat the school fly-fishing record by catching eighteen brown trout on a Tup's Indispensable and before breakfast, to come up and receive her award, this very handsome pair of fully rubberised Walton Waders, guaranteed split-proof'.

Well then, in those Common Entrance and other examinations which ensure a child's proper standard of achievement before admission, fishing will, I suppose, have to play its part, with periodical disappointments in the Practical Test — 'Frankly, Jennifer's casting is a dangerous disaster' and 'Brenda's flies were very poorly tied'.

Fishing is surely not the only possible hobby that is going to activate reluctant schoolchildren and one imagines that riding too will be included, with Mr Turnbull shouting, on this occasion, 'To the stables!' and, snatching up jodhpurs, curry combs, snaffles and a rosette or two, off they joyously go.

Here once more, never having even sat on a horse, let alone fallen off one, I am at a loss. What questions would one have to face in one's O Level Riding?

(a) Differentiate between saddle sores, girth galls and stable stains.

(b) There was once a famous horse called Dawn Wind. Why?

(c) Say everything that you know about hoof oil.

(d) Horses are sometimes said to have sloping shoulders, well let down hocks, plenty of feather on their legs, and massive quarters. Which of these are good?

And here again too, poor Miss Merridew, waving litmus paper and with her fume cupboards invitingly open, discovers, on asking for Gloria Westinghouse, that she is either practising her dressage or has come a purler at the double oxer and, badly concussed, is lying flat in the San.

On the other hand, the reply might be that she is 'schooling Moonbeam', perhaps the only thing on legs that will, in schools of the future, be properly schooled.

STOP PRESS

Not greatly caring at the moment for things as they are and life as it is, I am planning for the years ahead my very own home-made News Factory.

So copious and detailed have been the reviews of the important but largely disagreeable events of the last year which many newspapers saw fit to print prior to the joyous New Year, that they only succeeded in depressing us all over again.

I intend, therefore, to provide readers with various possible items for the next decade that are entirely unworrying and merely come under the heading of News That Couldn't Matter Less, though of course to be newsworthy each item has to be of a vaguely sensational or unusual nature.

How's this for starters?

MONA LISA SCOWLS

Leonardo's Revenge?

Louvre officials received a severe shock yesterday when, on opening up, they found the Mona Lisa no longer simpering but actually frowning at them in a markedly unpleasant manner. *'C'était une surprise très désagréable'* volunteered the uniformed oldster in whose *salle* the priceless picture hangs.

Experts think that wily Da Vinci, who had no love of the French, mixed into his colours a little-known but active pigment liable, in a few centuries, to violent chemical change, thus drastically altering the lady's expression.

Domestic news from the provinces is almost always fascinating.

107

HOME BANS CROQUET

Dangerous Sport

It started as a 'fun' game between Mesdames Dora Pritchard, 87, and Maud Scrumpton, 84, both residents at Merrymount Hall in the Waterbury Road, but tempers flared when Dora (blue and yellow) sent Maud (black and

But tempers flared when Dora . . . sent Maud . . . flying

red) flying into the herbaceous for the fourth time before pegging out and winning. Blows with mallets ensued, fortunately resulting in nothing worse than a few contusions.

'I have pulled up the hoops until they come to their senses,' firmly stated Matron Rumfield. 'For the time being, there's only going to be one way of "pegging out" here', she added with a twinkle. Game, set and match to you, Matron!

Back to France again for another blockbuster.

EIFFEL TOWER DISCREDITED

Height Falsified

The discovery that the Eiffel Tower is actually 2¼ feet lower than was once thought has set *tout Paris* talking. The tower's engineer, Alexandre Gustave Eiffel, who died as late as 1923, did not, however, take his guilty secret with him to the grave.

'My grandfather', recently claimed white-haired 'Gigi' Eiffel, sprightly bachelor and *boulevardier*, 'heard a rumour that a similar tower was under construction in, where else, Chicago, and, not wishing to be outdone, added on the extra and imaginary inches.' *Sale type, n'est-ce pas?*

A plan to increase the tower by 2¼ feet, even if only with a weather-cock or *girouette*, is said to be under discussion.

Some of our well-known public characters remain newsworthy all their lives and are bound to bob up sooner or later.

BROADSTAIRS MISHAP

Scout's Plucky Act

But for the instinctive action of Ernest Tusk, 13, of 'Chatsworth', Belvedere Crescent, holder of four swimming cups, an ex-Prime Minister would today be going hatless!

A sudden gust of wind swept Mr Heath's yachting cap into the sea as he was enjoying a 'cloudless' stroll along the Broadstairs 'front' and Ernest, plunging into the water that sometimes reached his shorts, retrieved the cherished headpiece.

The presentation of a framed Testimonial is being considered by the Town Council, but will the incident affect the young man's political opinions? Like Brer Fox, Ernest 'ain't sayin' nothin''.

It seems inconceivable that Russia will not feature prominently, and if so, why not like this?

MORE BALLET DEFECTIONS

Entire Bolshoi Here

The unexpected arrival at Covent Garden of the whole of the élite Russian ballet company, now seeking work permits, has met with a mixed reception in the famed *coulisses*. 'They can all jump higher than what we can', pouted our own petite little Toumarova Kandetski (née Dawn Pickthorn), 'but good luck to them, I say'. 'Most of us are hopping mad', quipped svelte Alexis Wemberov (Cyril Bagshawe), 'but just you wait till they find out the cost of caviare!'

It is understood that the majority of the ballet members were able to smuggle out their tutus.

And so on. How very unnerving if, as may well happen, some of these events actually turn out to be true.

CAN I HELP YOU?

A recent survey carried out among 1,000 shopgirls in large centres such as Birmingham and Manchester revealed that 88% of them preferred to serve male customers. The reasons given were that they argued less than women, said 'thank you' more often and were more patient, but the real basic reason, which was left unsaid, must surely be clear to all — the simple fact that male customers are men.

There is a long British tradition of harmless flirtation in the *va-et-vient* of the commercial world when members of the opposite sex meet together. In the happy days when there were teashops everywhere rather than hamburger joints, any young waitress worth her salt was ready with a 'Now then, Mr Cheeky!' when something more elaborate than toasted tea-cake was asked for. And, if that didn't shut the gentleman up, she gave him a sharp rap over the knuckles with her pencil.

Until the self-service rage began, almost everything concerning shops favoured romance. They tended to be dimly lit and to have a not displeasingly musty smell. Shopgirls may now foolishly prefer to be called 'female store assistants' (dotty of them to substitute the word 'female' for 'girl') or even, in the higher realms of fashion, *vendeuses*, a name with an in-built haughtiness about it.

But the very word 'shopgirl' used to suggest pure and impoverished little waifs, living on cocoa and 'Marie' biscuits in the geyserland of bed-sits, frail creatures much in need of masculine protection. They washed their hair on Fridays and wore it centrally parted in two swags or loops that swept back and terminated in a tasteful bun from which an occasional hairpin clattered to the floor.

And what an appealing picture they made in their white satin blouses timidly smiling from behind the counter, a wooden barrier which was itself a challenge to any hot-blooded male, for what are barriers for but to be torn down? Occasionally an imperious male floorwalker (remember those fellows?) would summon one of them out into, so to speak, the light of day ('Forward, please, Miss Jellaby') and a neatly turned ankle and foot became visible.

'Can I help you, sir?' The simple words, modestly uttered with just a hint of eyelid-flutter, won all men's hearts and the enterprising customer found it easy to move on from there to a closer acquaintance ('Excuse me, but usedn't you to be in Corsets?').

A sudden blush and then a quick shared chuckle might follow this unintentional impropriety, with the gentleman saying something merry like 'I say, I do seem to have put my silly old foot into the jolly old potage, don't I?'

Then, with the purchase made and, perhaps, fingers touching as the sum of four-and-eleven-three was handed over, the bill and the money were deftly inserted into a round metal capsule and excitingly fired along a wire to a raised central cash desk presided over by a commanding lady looking not unlike an Empress at a Durbar. A moment of suspense and then back the receipted bill came whizzing.

'Will that be all, sir?' It is now or never. 'Well, there was, er, something. I was just wondering . . .', and before long our two budding love-birds are enjoying tea-for-two at the Kardomah ('Do I see a little lady who can manage another fancy?').

Not for nothing was a famous musical comedy of seventy years ago, *Our Miss Gibbs* (as 'big' in its day as *Oklahoma* and *My Fair Lady*), set in a large store ('Garrods', I need hardly say) with its heroine a shopgirl, Mary Gibbs, and played by a not inconsiderable talent called Gertie Millar.

Miss Gibbs has many suitors (at times the shop is jammed with them all loudly singing) and the man of her choice (the incognito Lord Enysford, son and heir to the Earl of St Ives, you know) warbles what is in all their hearts:

Can I help you?

There's a girl at the Stores called Mary,
She's dainty and rather demure,
I come ev'ry day, I can't keep away,
There's nobody like her, I'm sure.

No indeed. And where, may I ask, is she now? Gone are the mahogany counters (and those useful little chairs that one could rest awhile on). No more are there Empresses at Durbars or those whizzing capsules (except on the Moon). Gone are the demure smiles. Absent are the floorwalkers. Vanished are the Misses Jellaby. I cannot for the life of me imagine how they were able to round up as many as a thousand shopgirls for that survey. In stores one now increasingly fends for oneself — a sad encouragement to the daily hordes of oriental shoplifters — preparatory to queuing up at a square enclosure rather brusquely labelled PAY HERE. Gone too the whispered 'Can I help you, sir?' I suppose that Heaven helps those who, like the orientals, help themselves.

TING-A-LING

It was Somerset Maugham who first pointed out, in *Cakes and Ale*, that when you get a telephone message asking you to ring somebody and adding that the matter is urgent, the matter is likely to be a more urgent one for him than for you. Therefore you can safely bide your time.

Although I no longer climb, dripping, out of the bath to answer it ('Is that Debenhams?'), it requires a strength of character which I do not possess to ignore the telephone's insistent ting-a-ling. Long since gone are those happy days when an operator in the exchange plugged you in and worked your bell in a languid and merciful manner while she (for a she it always was) sipped cocoa and buffed her nails.

Older readers may well recall the time when such telephonists were admired objects of mystery and romance, their sweetly modulated tones building up a picture of a comely auburn beauty perched confidently at her controls and cooing away down the wires ('I have Cowes on the line').

Song-writers wrote lyrics about them, bewailing the fact that their lips were pressed to the telephone rather than being active elsewhere. Novelists wrote novels (*The Siren of the Switchboard*, her panel vibrant with passion). Who can doubt that the 1920s style of hair, plaited and coiled like a small table-mat and then clamped firmly to the ears, was in envious imitation of the telephonists' headphones ('Speak up, Devizes!'). Charm was their stock-in-trade but they knew how to handle cheeky chat, with a 'Kindly press your Button B, Mr Saucyboots. No, I cannot do it for you'.

Then the telephone was an excitement, sparingly used. Impossible to deny that nowadays most calls are in some way bothersome. How unwelcome are those 'surprise' calls beginning with 'You'll never guess who this is' from a female voice sounding coy. 'No can do? Well, do you remember a tiny wee

114

scrap of a thing who in 1927 lived next door to you in Reading?' It seems that the wee scrap has become altogether larger, now calls itself Trish McLoomis ('My hubb's in metal boxes') and longs to renew acquaintance ('We're throwing a cheese-and-wine on the 18th . . .').

And it cannot be long to the final horror — a television screen attached to the apparatus revealing Trisha McLoomis herself, cheerily beaming and in the full glory of Luxiephone Supercolour.

But, for those who are anti-telephone, help is available from two quarters — the canine world and an American computer centre. I read that a delightful lady who has a way with dogs and other animals has demonstrated how she taught her Great Dane to run a vacuum cleaner over the sitting-room carpet. It also learnt how to answer the telephone, delicately lifting the receiver in its jaws, barking an acknowledgement ('I will see if she is in') and fetching help. Whether or not it then dusted the sideboard and baked a batch of Danish fancies I do not know but it appears likely.

This is fine for those with Great Danes, but we have a West Highland terrier from a proud Scottish strain. It is a charming dog but sadly lacking in any sense of obligation as regards household chores other than nipping the postman. If allowed access to a telephone, he would at once chew through the wires. Shown a vacuum cleaner in action, he would promptly bite its bag.

But from our other source comes news that any minute now a device will be obtainable that can recognise the telephone numbers of incoming calls and only allow those through that are on the subscriber's 'Happy Hello List', which in my case would be all of nine persons. And later in the day it provides details of those callers whom it has shunned.

What nicer bedtime reading could there possibly be prior to sinking, profoundly relieved to have missed all that jabber ('How's that poor old leg of yours?'), into Dreamland?

FACING FACTS

FACING FACTS

Those of us who are, or have been, privileged to review, possibly for a variety of newspapers and magazines, biographical and autobiographical books can probably all report the same unexpectedly rich crop of Astounding Facts that they have harvested and with which to enliven, or more likely silence, dinner table conversations. I have been so reviewing for fifty years and can therefore claim my share of startling information.

You'll appreciate examples. Very well. Did you know that the famous dietician, W. Banting, was himself so stout that he could only safely proceed downstairs backwards, that Brahms's stepmother was a cook called Schnack, and that, following complaints, the Bishop of Colchester's cat, 'Sherry', was hurriedly re-named 'Shandy' as being a less strong and damaging intoxicant?

More? Have you ever realised that it was not fruit that Nell Gwynne sold but herrings, that Peter Townsend once had, as in some frightful nightmare, to teach Queen Mary how to dance the Hokey Cokey, and that Bette Davis's mother liked to be called Fred?

Then, is it, one wonders, at all widely known that the shooting of the Korda film about Nelson was held up because nobody could remember which arm it was that he lost, that the name of the very first Miss Singapore was Violet Wee, and that the inventor of a kite-drawn bath-chair once went on a windy day whizzing through Chippenham at an estimated 25 m.p.h.?

Meatier chunks of fact follow, one's heartfelt admiration going out to those authors who have so diligently dug and delved and disinterred such a wealth of eyebrow-raising material.

NEAR MISSES

(*The Book of Heroic Failures* by Stephen Pile)

It is, I think, only the British who have a soft spot for failures. In Russia they are, presumably, put down salt mines. Americans worship nothing but success. In France, also-rans are treated with contempt, but here we often greatly prefer them to the winners.

Take, for example, the fifty Mexican convicts who dug an escape tunnel out of their jail and surfaced in the very court-room where many of them had been sentenced ('Hullo again!'). And, although this hardly ranks as a failure, there was a lady in Fiji who took 34 years to complete a *Times* crossword. Then what can one make of the extremely petite and light girl para-chutist who, when she jumped in the slightest of winds, went not down but up?

One has one's favourites in this splendid panorama of non-achievement. In 1973, a fire engine caught fire and, although carrying 400 gallons of water at the time, was unable to put itself out. In 1971, a Margate couple on holiday in Wales joined a BR mystery tour which took them straight back to Margate ('We nearly fell through the platform'). And rather touching was the case of The Worst Homing Pigeon. This historic bird was released in Pembrokeshire in 1953 and was expected to reach its base that evening. No sign of it, however, until eleven years later when it was returned by parcel post from Brazil, dead and in a cardboard box. 'We had quite given it up for lost', its owner said.

Now that hijacking has become so popular, it will be hard to beat the record of the man who, in 1976 and during a flight across America, took the stewardess hostage, waving a gun. 'Take me to Detroit', he demanded. 'We're already going to Detroit', she replied. Collapse, as *Punch* jokes used to say, of hijacker. Those whose married life has not been prolonged will marvel at the Sluckins of Kensington, who remained in a state of marital bliss for precisely one hour, after which the lady announced that she 'had a few doubts' and left for the Divine Light Meditation Commune in Finchley.

My prize choice goes to Miss 'Rita Thunderbird', a lady who makes a profession from being fired out of a cannon as a human cannon-ball and who, on one occasion, remained firmly inside the cannon while the explosive power blew her bra right across the River Thames.

While the explosive power blew her bra right across the River Thames

MAN-TRAPS

(*The Dollar Princesses* by Ruth Brandon)

Miss Brandon's history of the female American invasion of the European male aristocracy between 1870 and 1914 bristles with facts to cherish. An annual New York publication called *Titled Americans* listed, in 1915, the impressive total of 454 American women who had, with their fathers' cheque books at the ready, crossed the Atlantic to some social purpose. It was usually a purely business arrangement and Dan Cupid twanged his bow on sadly few occasions.

Countesses preponderated (136 in all), with 42 princesses, 17 duchesses, 33 marchionesses and assorted small fry, and in this splendidly rich, in every sense, field, Miss Brandon wisely concentrates on some of the most interesting nuptials.

Take, for example, the woefully plain Anna Gould (her father's fortune was based on the manufacture of a spectacularly successful mouse-trap) who had, I regret to say, long black hairs all down her back and a swarthy face that would not have caused comment if seen peering out of a wigwam. She netted the fascinating and blond-whiskered Marquis Boni de Castellane who gritted his teeth and fathered three sons, receiving in return three million dollars, access to Anna's fifteen million, and a bed that had belonged to Marie Antoinette.

On Boni's proving alarmingly unfaithful, intrepid Anna set her sights even higher and secured the Prince de Sagan, a spirited chap who, finding the Prince of Wales in bed with his mother, removed all the royal clothes and threw them into the nearest fountain. Meanwhile the mouse-trap (can it have been called The Little Nipper?) clicked away and everybody was happy.

Splendidly triumphant too were the Singers (sewing-machines). *La veuve Singer* hooked up with a French duke, while her daughter, Winnaretta, who had improbably spent all her youth in Paignton, married, in succession, two princes, even though rather preferring ladies to gentlemen.

The going rate for English dukes was about three million and it must be said for the man-hunters that they kept their side of the bargain and stumped nobly up. Consuelo Marlborough re-leaded Blenheim's fourteen acres of roofs, installed central heating, and put up with a boudoir in sight of a pond in which an ex-butler had committed suicide.

Occasionally there was a true love match, notably Mary Leiter, daughter of a prosperous storekeeper and of a mother given to malapropisms ('My husband is going to the fancy dress ball in the garbage of a monk'), who, brushing aside the Count of Turin and the Marchese Rudini, fell head over heels in love with the austere and then untitled Curzon, and he, eventually, with her. The heart warms.

Even damaged English goods were marketable and, on the very day that he was cashiered from the Scots Guards for the Tranby Croft scandal, Sir William Gordon-Cunningham married the delightfully rich Miss Garner.

And on to the nearly present day and Maude Burke who married, though in love with George Moore, Sir Bache Cunard, a ship owner so besotted with her that he fashioned for her a decorative gate in fancy ironwork and with the words 'Come into the garden Maud' picked out in horse-shoes. Could love go further?

Maud turned herself into Emerald, the bouncy London hostess whom Lady Cynthia Asquith described as 'looking more like an inebriated canary than ever'. But Emerald could be highly comical, as when introducing Michael Arlen as 'the only Armenian who hasn't been massacred'.

123

WE DON'T WANT TO LOSE YOU

(*Dear Old Blighty* by E. S. Turner)

Every year the appalling idiocies (and I mean no disrespect to those who so bravely and so unproductively died) of the First World War become more apparent. While women reservists learnt, wildly waving, how to semaphore (but what, and to whom?) and parliament debated whether a winkle could rightly be called a fish, 37 million casualties piled up and the Hapsburgs (who was it called them the Perhapsburgs?) and the Hohenzollerns and the Romanovs vanished, moodily or violently, into oblivion.

Atrocity stories kept hatred of the Hun at boiling point (Belgian breasts cut off, and nuns hung head downwards as clappers for bells, were both very popular items) and the country agitated itself about German names. The Bechstein piano firm was hastily sold off to Debenhams, Boots rushed out a British version of *eau de Cologne* (*eau de Bournemouth?*), and Royal Worcester Corsets relentlessly pursued sellers of corsets suspected of being German. People called Rosenheim became overnight Rose, and Schwabacher, Shaw.

In the early days, the phantom Russian expeditionary force cheered everybody up no end. It was said to have landed in Scotland, entrained and then swept south to our aid. Russians had been seen at Carlisle swigging vodka, and at Durham they had jammed roubles into slot-machines. Pausing awhile at Crewe, a group of four had taken advantage of a landlady, an activity which presumably dislodged at least some of the snow on their boots.

In the interests of manpower, something very like the old press gangs were formed to round up shirkers and they pounced here and there — the Ring at Blackfriars, Newmarket Race-course, Hull football ground and whist drives at Tottenham. Even when safely in the army, nobody was safe from grave questions of etiquette. Officers were one thing, privates another (after 1917 *The Times* listed fallen officers only) and so what on earth were the poor Baden-Powells to do when their chauffeur returned commissioned as a 'TG' or Temporary Gentleman?

Against a background of daily horror — the agonising telegrams, the mounting casualties, the street shrines, the Zeppelins, the bad (for some) food — almost anything could happen. A Derby woman secondhand clothes dealer was accused of trying to further the suffragettes' cause by inserting poisoned nails into Lloyd George's boots and, if those failed, he was to be picked off with a poisoned dart on Walton Heath golf course.

How extraordinary that in 1915 there were conducted tours of the battlefields ('Heads!') and that the rich could throughout the war visit the French Riviera, advertisements of 1917 reading 'Where to Winter: Monte Carlo'. Meanwhile, widows of private soldiers got the princely sum of 5/- a week, and Lord Lonsdale's economies included disbanding his own orchestra.

The O.B.E. citation lists (it was derisively known as 'Order of the Bad Egg', among other things) provide some strange answers to the question 'What did YOU do in the Great War, Daddy?' Daddy might have lent his home for a hospital, 'worked late on HMSO accounts', inspected prisoner-of-war parcels, been a typist in Norway, or 'originated the use of goat-skins in the British Army'. And an M.B.E. was lavished on a lady who remained defiantly at her lathe with a broken thumb.

LIST AWHILE

(*The Book of Royal Lists* by Craig Brown and Lesley Cunliffe)

A suitable sub-title for this book would be All You Wanted to Know about Royal Families But Were Too Embarrassed to Ask, not that many fresh embarrassments lurk within (Prince Philip's merry gaffes and jokes are well known to us, though less familiar is his comment, while in Holland, on his hosts: 'What a po-faced lot these Dutch are!').

The information is offered in tidy list form — Sixteen Kings Who Sired Bastards: Six Fashion Hints from Royalty ('A woman can never be too rich or too thin' — The Duchess of Windsor): Eighteen Dislikes of Queen Victoria, among them bishops, cars, 'education for the working classes' and children, her own most of all and with Edward VII getting it in the neck: 'Handsome I cannot think him, with those immense features and total want of chin . . . Dull and ignorant, I never can look at him without a shudder'. Our own Queen's alleged dislikes seem tame by comparison — ivy, Dickens, grouse, edible snails and Wimbledon.

Various isolated titbits might have the heading 'Oh Really?' Prince Philip was born in a house called 'Mon Repos'. Anne Boleyn had three breasts and an extra finger. At Windsor Queen Victoria economised on lavatory paper and substituted back numbers of *The Times*. George V was tattooed by a Japanese. On a Jamaican visit the Queen was allotted a beach hut called 'Kosy Korna'.

Royal senses of humour tend to be different from those of some of us and in a list which should have been headed 'How We Roared!' we hear tell of tadpole sandwiches, whoopee cushions at Sandringham (especially hilarious when a bishop sank down on one), live lobsters in beds and exploding cigars.

There are Four Aspects of Life on which Royalty Has Been Ignorant (Queen Mary got her first sight of hay at wartime Badminton and when she was seventy-two, gasping out 'Oh, *that's* what hay looks like!') and particularly pleasing is the story of Queen Alexandra muddling golf with croquet and, when on the green, gaily hitting her husband's golf-ball away from the hole and then pushing her own in. I looked, but in vain, for a list of Swear-Words Used by Kings.

RUMMY OLD PLACE

(*The House: A Portrait of Chatsworth* by the Duchess of Devonshire)

High up in Derbyshire and roughly in the middle of England stands what must the country's most beautiful house, 'a very big house in a very big valley' and the home of the Cavendish family.

Constant alterations and embellishments have been going on since the first house in 1552, where the unsatisfactory Mary Queen of Scots was a temporary and grumpy guest. The first Duke rebuilt the old house in 1686 'at a time when it was impossible to invent anything ugly'. The second Duke stuffed the place with important prints and engravings and drawings. The third Duke acquired two Van Dycks and the fourth altered the course of the River Derwent and instructed James Paine to provide new stables and that superb bridge, while Capability Brown laid out the park.

The fifth Duke's chief contribution was to marry the famous Georgiana and to father the immensely jolly sixth Duke, an unexplained bachelor. He had the luck to coincide with Joseph Paxton, who provided the Great Conservatory, the peach houses and vineries and who devised the stupendous waterworks and cascades and fountains. The Duke also found time to write, in 1844, his charming *Handbook to Chatsworth*.

The seventh Duke struggled rather unsuccessfully with appallingly large inherited debts (not the last to have to do so), while the eighth, whiskery 'Harty-Tarty', served Parliament for half a century and, defiantly absent-minded, invited the King to dine at Devonshire House and then forgot to turn up. 'An American lady who went into ecstasies over the beauties of Chatsworth was greatly disconcerted when he answered, "It's a rummy old place".' Meanwhile, as down the years valuable acquisitions have poured in at one door, saleable possessions have poured out of another and into the grasping hands of the death duty fiends and their vulgar clamourings for eighty per cent of the proceeds.

The house has been open for people to see round since it was built and the present Duke and Duchess have struggled, nobly indeed, to preserve and improve the countless beauties of the place. We could hardly have, for *The House*, a better guide than the Duchess and one doubts whether Chatsworth has ever had a prettier, wittier or more conscientious landlady. Fun and jokes are everywhere. Sitting to Annigoni for a portrait, she found herself apologising ('I know it's not the kind you like') for her face. 'He made an Italian gesture of resignation and said "Oh well, it doesn't matter. It's not your fault".' She decided to hang a chandelier near the painting of *The Rape of the Sabines* ('It seemed to cheer up the rapists and the raped').

How fascinating to find that in the early 1900s all guests at the house were weighed on arrival and the visitors' books recorded the sometimes gloomy results. Then there are the carvings in the Oak Room ('Some look like mad Boy Scouts') and the titles for the false book-backs which cover a door in the library: *Sideways Through Derbyshire* by Crabbe: *Alien Corn* by Dr Scholl: *Consenting Adults* by Abel N. Willing.

EMPTY CUPBOARD

(*John Buchan and his World* by Janet Adam Smith)

'I cannot believe', says John Buchan in his own rather thin and unrevealing autobiography, *Memory Hold-the-Door*, 'that the external incidents of my life are important enough to be worth chronicling in detail'. This has not been the view of Miss Janet Adam Smith.

There can never have been such a success story. Nothing ever went wrong for him. The son, born in 1875, of a minister of the John Knox Free Church of Scotland who preached the Gospel at street corners, he had an impeccably unprivileged and non-affluent childhood and youth at Hutcheson's Grammar School (two miles from the Gorbals) and made his way thence by scholarships to Glasgow University, where Gilbert Murray gave him extra tutorials and considered him 'a treasure of a pupil'. And so to Brasenose and Oxford in 1895. Even at this relatively early age, stories and articles were being published, and paid for, in *The Gentleman's Magazine*.

'Everything he put his hand to prospered', a Glasgow contemporary wrote of Buchan. 'He believed in himself, not offensively, but with a quiet reserve. He had an air of simple and convincing assurance'. He certainly convinced Oxford — a classical scholarship, President of the Union, and a First in greats. He read for the Bar, he wrote regularly for the *Spectator*, he published his early novels, he assisted Lord Milner, then High Commissioner of South Africa, to tidy up there after the Boer War ('I don't like him', was his first opinion of Cecil Rhodes, 'but he is undoubtedly a great man'). He disliked African towns but fell hook, line and sinker for the veldt which, with its jagged blue mountains so reminiscent of the Coolins, and its streams and long green glens, was to have such a powerful influence on his writing and produced *Prester John*.

Back in London at the Bar and by now something of a social catch and in great demand for country-house weekends, he had the good fortune to meet and marry Susan Grosvenor, grand-daughter of Lord Ebury and through her parents related to Westminsters and Wellingtons, to Lovelaces, Lytteltons and Talbots, and it is at about this point (and it is no fault of Miss Adam Smith) that one starts to long for some sort of skeleton in the cupboard — tipsy incarcerations in Vine Street, Soho indiscretions, vast gambling debts or a torrid affair at Oxford with a tobacconist's daughter (always at great risk in the undergraduate world of that day). No such luck. What could one expect of somebody, old long before his time, who found his fellow Oxonians 'over-grown schoolboys, immature and rowdy'?

The happy marriage and honeymoon provided only a momentary hiccough in the steady onward march of events. He inaugurated (and how grateful we should be) the Nelson Sixpenny classics and the Sevenpenny Library of popular reprints (Wells, Henry James, Conrad, and so on). He wrote *The Thirty-Nine Steps*. He was Director of Intelligence in Beaverbrook's new Ministry of Information. There were fishing holidays in the Highlands and Norway. The Buchan nursery filled up (how did he find the time, one wonders?) and he bought the, for him, ideal country house, Elsfield Manor, near Oxford (the opening pages of *The Three Hostages* describe it, in a style that some may find complacent).

And on yet again to election as MP for the Scottish Universities, various academic honours, the CH, a new novel every year and, not surprisingly, a duodenal ulcer. And finally, and no life ended with less of an anti-climax, Governor General of Canada and Baron Tweedsmuir, dying in Canada from a cerebral thrombosis in 1940.

Obviously a very good and kind and conscientious and generous man and a gifted historian and storyteller, so what then is wrong and why has one reader at least some reservations about him? It is, I think, the relentless calculation with which all this was achieved. From his undergraduate days it was his custom to write out a 'List of Things to be Done'. This included a section called 'Honours Gained and to be Gained', one of which, Fellow of All Souls, eluded him. This is very off-putting. To paraphrase Lady Bracknell, an honour should come upon a young man as a surprise, pleasant or unpleasant as the case may be. The items scheduled among the plans for 1919 include settling in Elsfield, publishing *Mr Standfast* and 'LL.D and KCB'. Oh dear oh dear. How agreeable it would have been to find that he had perhaps once, in moonstruck mood, done something wild and risky and frivolous and unforeseen and just for the hell of it. Can it be that he was totally without humour? The books would seem to suggest so.

THE URGE TO SEE SERGE

(De Basil's Ballets Russes by Kathrine Sorley Walker)

Strange indeed is the wide variety of things and people which the inhabitants of these islands suddenly decide to clasp to their bosoms and cherish for evermore — Stonehenge, scampi, Lord Hailsham, barbecues, loft ladders, Anna Neagle, fish fingers, grubby jeans, Virginia Wade — and almost the most unexpected of the lot, given our well-known British suspicion of anything 'artistic', is the hold that ballet, and especially our home-grown kind, has had on the public in the last fifty or so years. Whoever would have thought that our stolid race could ever produce such a galaxy as that composed of de Valois, Ashton, Fonteyn, Helpmann, Dowell, Sibley and many others?

Not that ballet caught on straight away or was welcomed with equal enthusiasm in all parts of the country. There was the merry episode on her first visit to Edinburgh when Pavlova, touring with her company and nearing the end of her famous Dying Swan dance, was spread-eagled upon the stage, a white feathered form twitching and fluttering her life out to that memorable music: a moving moment and a sturdy Scottish lady was heard to say loudly to her neighbour, 'You know, she reminds me a little of Mrs McCracken'.

Even in the '30s and in London, where the main crop of balletomanes was to be found, comediennes were still indulging in comic take-offs (they usually called themselves something witty such as Olga Toppleova) and there was Farjeon's affectionate send-up song, 'When Bolonsky Danced Belushka in September 1910'.

> Oh, the urge
> To see Serge!
> What a thrill!
> What a pill!
> What a purge!

That supreme performer, Hermione Baddeley, dressed in a long, mauve and shapeless sack and wearing a lot of rattling necklaces and beads, led a quartet of fans in a nostalgic memory of that great 1910 night:

> How we screamed and shrieked and hooted,
> How we wooped and how we howled!
> We were ravished and uprooted!
> We were frankly disembowelled!

Miss Baddeley, never one to underplay a valuable line, did full justice to the final word.

Farjeon's 'Belushka' was, of course, a joky corruption of the Diaghilev ballet *Petrouchka*, choreography by Fokine to the music of Stravinsky, Diaghilev's company having already appeared frequently at Covent Garden and elsewhere; and it was to London that, in 1933, an émigré Cossack officer called Colonel de Basil brought his Monte Carlo-recruited ballet company, a company which, in view of its component parts, had every right to call itself the Ballets Russes. Although many dancers adopt other, and generally Slavonic, names (Eva Hartwig prudently swopped it for Vera Zorina, Valrene Tweedie very wisely became Irina Lavrova, and our own treasured Dame Margot kicked off in life as Peggy Hookham), the Colonel had decided on the opposite process, his original Russian name, which need not concern us here, being lengthy and, in the west, a bit of a tongue-twister.

Londoners, robbed for four years of foreign balletic treats by the death of Diaghilev in 1929, pounced eagerly on the new arrivals. They came, under the wing of Sir Oswald Stoll, into the vast Alhambra, home of *The Bing Boys* and George Robey. It did not matter. They could, as far as the public minded, have performed in an ABC tea-shop and what was at first intended to be a three-week season extended itself triumphantly from July to November. Led by the great Russian and former Diaghilev stars, Massine and Danilova (for many, still the most magical of them all), the dancers included three so-called 'baby ballerinas', Baronova, Riabouchinska and Toumanova, each of them to become, before many more *fouettés* were out, a *prima ballerina assoluta*. There were ballets by Fokine, Massine and Balanchine. The orchestra was conducted by Efrem Kurtz. The Savoy Grill advertised special Russian dishes and down the red lanes of those who could afford them the tasty blinis slithered. Could appreciation go further? De Basil was made.

He had done well, and by 1932, to assemble such an array of talent for, after Diaghilev's death, not only were the dancers widely dispersed but also sadly scattered were the costumes and décors with which to mount the great ballets on which the company at first mainly depended — *Les Sylphides*, *La Boutique Fantasque*, *Prince Igor*, *Scheherazade* and the rest of them, a repertory of over twenty. Many of these would have benefited from the presence in the cast of a distinguished *danseur noble*, a Nijinsky or a Nureyev, but such phenomena are rare and they had to get by on the strength of their male *demi-caractère* performers, headed by Lichine and Woizikovsky and, of course, the masterly Massine.

Lucky enough to have the help of René Blum as the Monte Carlo artistic director and to have that enchanting Casino theatre as rehearsal room and show-case and base, the extraordinary Colonel, for whom intrigue, scheming, double-dealing, sharp practice and blazing rows were the very stuff of life and who knew little or nothing of ballet, managed to keep the whole crazy raft afloat, partly by means of his great charm and partly by the iron rod. His contracts hardly favoured the dancers. Classes were obligatory and absences incurred heavy fines. Rehearsal clothes were to be invariably 'ladies in a black Greek tunic, men in black trousers and white shirts'. Men must shave off beards and moustaches as required. No drinking or smoking in the theatre and de Basil's word was final. Svelte and slim figures were encouraged to remain so by the meagre nature of the pay-packet.

As ballet dancers are by nature masochistic and rather enjoy being bullied by somebody they respect (it is said that even now, when de Valois is known to be in front, they all shiver in their shoes), de Basil was admired rather than disliked. Primitive living conditions seemed also to fit into the picture. Toumanova, who was everybody's idea of a ballerina (huge, dark eyes, raven hair and magnolia skin), has revealed that, in London, she lived on fish and chips warmed up on a gas ring in a Seven Dials attic. Small and dingy hotels housed the rest, and how touching to find them taking their hols at The Balmoral Hotel, Torquay. The girls could afford no jewellery and de Basil's company, although fêted, was not as successful socially as Diaghilev's had been.

How well our authoress describes the inner fires that drove these dancers on:

> The company's devotion to the dance triumphed over everything. This is a point that cannot be overstressed. The commitment of dancers in the 'thirties, dancers of all nationalities, to ballet was total. Their belief in it as a vocation affected every aspect of their lives . . . They cared so passionately about ballet that to dance, even in small roles, in the *corps de ballet*, was a privilege. To work with choreographers such as Fokine, Balanchine, Massine or Nijinska they were willing to forego financial return, to scrape along on a pittance, to work all hours of the day or night, well or ill, in any conditions.

It would be quite inaccurate to consider, as many do, stage performers as being vain. When they talk, they tell not of triumphs but of disasters, of missed entrances, forgotten lines and of speeches boomed out by mistake an act too soon. Ballet dancers are no exception and even Dame Ninette has a misfortune to report:

> I had an entrance with Danilova, both of us completely hidden in Lotus leaves which, upon the slight pulling of strings inside loosening the walls of our prison, fell about us as a form of extra skirt. On we both came, whirling, and on I continued to whirl until the end, like a mad white cabbage, for my leaves had refused to fall, and so I remained imprisoned for the entire performance, guided about the stage by the frenzied whispers of Danilova.

On one occasion, Massine's dog, Smokey, came leaping on with the fiercely prancing warriors in *Prince Igor*, while a terrier puppy of Rostova's was happy to join the ladies during *Les Sylphides*. And it was at Bournemouth that Rostova, mercifully undamaged, went too near a candle and caught fire in the wings, subsequently rushing on stage merrily alight, a sharp-eyed reporter from the *Bournemouth Daily Echo* neatly summing it all up ('The incident was the talk of the building').

The story has, alas, no happy ending. The Colonel's Ballets Russes folded finally in 1952 and de Basil died a pauper. In quite good company, when one comes to think of it.

WEEKLY WISDOM

(*Great-Grandmama's Weekly* by Wendy Forrester)

The weekly concerned is *The Girl's Own Paper* from its beginning in 1880 to 1901, published by the Religious Tract Society and costing, pious tone and all, a mere penny.

Hot cakes hardly describes the way it sold (a circulation of over 250,000 in next to no time), and the first Editorial of all set out its aims — 'to be to the girls a Counsellor, Playmate, Guardian, Instructor, Companion and Friend' and, tall order though all that may sound, the pages here chosen fully justify the editor's claim.

Health was taken care of by an ex-naval doctor who is keen on 'perfumed' cod-liver oil and the use of chest expanders (Fig 4 in the illustrated and explanatory chart sets the pulses racing) and who also contributes thoughtful articles ('Why Am I So Pale?'). Nor does he shirk answering questions and 'Fatima of Smyrna' gets a tremendous ticking off for using belladonna (enlarged pupils). However, softening a little, he helps 'Mistletoe Maggie' with her blushing, and instructs 'Pa's Darling', whose complaint is not specified, 'to rub eyebrows three or four times a day with a piece of raw onion'.

The answers in the general correspondence column ('Your letter is a disgrace') tend to be sharp ('Your writing is quite the ugliest we have ever seen') and pulls no punches ('Are you out of your mind?'), with even a peer's daughter getting it in the neck for being 'careless and boasting'. So much so that the writers mostly sheltered behind pseudonyms such as 'Mad Cricketer' and 'Distressed Crumpet'.

Clothes are, naturally, not neglected. Clean those old coloured silks with six quarts or so of potato water, and no newly married girl should dream of embarking on Life's Mystery Tour with fewer than nine pairs of calico combinations. Brides should equip themselves with nine nightdresses, a pair of white 'bridal' corsets, and a navy serge boating dress. The answer to the article 'What Do You Do With A Wedding Dress' is not what you might think (take it off) but adapt it — veil the bodice with black lace and add a velveteen train — for that informal tea-party.

Brides should equip themselves with nine nightdresses, a pair of white 'bridal' corsets . . .

Not all is advice and instruction and there are several ('Only a Girl-Wife') gripping serials. What must have been an especially good fictional treat is the one in which the heroine insists on becoming a masseuse, the yarn's tasteful title being 'Kathleen's Handful'.

There's just so much else — How To Play The Harp, a plug for Morton's Patent Steam-Washing Machine, a girl who wants to know whether 'eating eggs and wearing high-heeled shoes makes you deaf', a plucky little child of eight rescuing her governess, Miss Bradshaw, from a pond, a reminder to take a whistle with you when tricycling, and advice on *not* being a lady organist ('strain on the loins').

As to class, there seems to be little doubt about the stratum aimed at. The clothes articles and illustrations reveal all, and there is even a piece of advice about How To Treat Female Servants: 'Be very kind but very strict. Remember they are merely grown-up children and treat them accordingly'. Even a penny was, for most, beyond the reach of the scullery and still-room.

CARRY ON BREEDING

(Little Princes by Sue Arnold)

From William the Conqueror to the exciting events in the Wales household, *Little Princes* follows the royal babies from conception, birth and early years through to their education, if any. William I, for example, was illiterate, having had bad luck with his tutors: the first two were poisoned and the last two were stabbed, one of them while actually in bed with his blood-soaked charge. 'It was not an atmosphere conducive to higher education' says Ms Arnold, who throughout pounces gleefully on any piquant happenings in our extremely rum past.

There was a great to-do about barren wives, and medieval midwives recommended a stew containing, amongst other mouth-waterers, boiled puppy. Further useful hints included crushed sage, honey and wood-ash (apply to the soles of the feet before turning in on Saturdays) while occasionally a mustard and sage bath taken at the full moon had been known to work the trick.

James II's poor old Queen Mary, woefully childless, popped on a swimsuit of primrose yellow satin and gingerly lowered herself into the Bath waters while an Italian string orchestra scraped out patriotic melodies (don't bother to try this one: quite hopeless).

Even when positively *enceinte*, royal people just carried on regardless, some continuing to hunt when well into their ninth month. When eight months gone, Catherine of Aragon's mother girded on her armour and rode into battle, while George III's Queen Charlotte danced on until the very last moment, and Queen Alexandra skated on the very day that her disastrous firstborn, Eddy, appeared.

Privacy was unknown. At St James's it was nothing for there to be sixty-seven in the royal bedchamber at a birth, 'all jostling for prime viewing space', and in France it was no better, Marie Antoinette getting goggled at by anybody who had drifted in and had a spare five minutes to kill.

You'll want to know the result of the Fertility Stakes. Easily first (or 'Top Royal Rabbit') was the aforesaid gavotte-mad Charlotte who produced fifteen children in twenty-one years, beating by a distance Edward III's Queen Philippa's seven sons and five daughters. The strongly fancied Victoria and Albert squeezed, with nine, into third place. Queen Charlotte, in the winner's enclosure, welcomed the public in groups of forty, treating them, between peeps at Our Latest, to seed cake and mock-zabaglione. Feminists will regret to hear that there was a time when the birth of a princess was on a par with a defeat in the World Cup.

Fascinating facts are everywhere. Christenings could be pretty tough (total immersion in Jordan water preceded by salting and oiling and, in Scotland, a spoonful of whisky) and for Charles II's baptism the congregation was requested to dress in crimson and white 'like something out of a Busby Berkeley musical'.

There, appropriate or not names were supplied, the Phillips' questionable 'Zara' sounding to Ms Arnold 'like the winner of the three-thirty at Lingfield'.

SIMPLY ROLLING, MY DEAR!

(*The Rich Rich* by Alan Jenkins)

Nowadays, few British or American people can afford, so to speak, to be rich, but not so many years ago, wealthy eccentrics flourished. Lord Berners had a piano built into his Rolls-Royce. The late Aly Khan, playing golf on a French course, tipped his girl caddy with a two-seater car. The 3rd Marquess of Hertford owned a large house and property in Wales which he had never seen but where, in case he should drop in, a huge dinner was prepared every night. Philip Sassoon, missing a train, summoned the stationmaster and said 'Bring me another'. Thomas Lipton (tea) imported the largest cheese in the world (it weighed five tons) and tried to press it on an extremely startled Queen Victoria ('Take it away!').

Across the Atlantic, Mr Potter Palmer (hotels) loaded his wife with so many diamonds that she became top-heavy and kept tumbling over, and you could always recognise Mrs Caroline Astor from behind as jewellery was dotted all the way down her spine (she had to sit bolt upright. Leaning against anything was agony). Jim Brady was lavish with gifts of gold-plated bicycles, and Ned Green enjoyed the somewhat rare luxury of a diamond-studded chamberpot.

Mr Jenkins has wisely concentrated on the way they spent their money. We don't want to hear about the early Vanderbilts plying for hire as boatmen on the eastern seaboard but it's fun to know, when the dollars came rolling in, how idiotically they got rid of them. And incidentally, what kind of wealth are we talking about? Well, at the age of twenty-one, Vincent Astor inherited money that brought him in 10,000 dollars *a day*. That kind.

You'll want to know, of course, the batting order of the Croesus First XI as far as we can judge it and looking back over the years. I estimate the following: Rothschilds, Vanderbilts, Guggenheims, Carnegies, Krupps, Sassoons, Rockefellers,

Fords, Astors, Gulbenkian, Onassis. Twelfth man: Paul Getty.

If one were rich, I think it is the minor treats that would be so enjoyable. In life, however, it is plainly mainly the major treats that have so besotted the well-lined. Yachts and houses, for instance. When it came to building really hideous houses, there was nobody to touch the Vanderbilts. The Astors might put up unsuitable French châteaux on the edge of New York's Central Park but the Vanderbilts, employing 600 workmen for a year and a half, erected a palace on 5th Avenue whose ballroom was an exact replica of Versailles.

Even the Vanderbilt 'summer cottage' at Newport had a hall forty-five feet high, eighty-two rooms and a front door that weighed seventy tons. The Walsh family (goldmines) of Washington, chummy with King Leopold of the Belgians and hoping for a royal visit, had a throne room built into their vast mansion, the throne shooting up out of the floor at the touch of a button, in the manner of a Wurlitzer cinema organ.

And, socially, everybody in America knew exactly where they were, and that's always so convenient. The Astors had gone up a class by moving their money out of trade (furs) and into property, which was considered more respectable. The Vanderbilts, still stuck in trade (transportation), could not 'know' the Astors, nor could they buy boxes on the plushiest tier at the opera (they settled this little problem by building an opera house of their own).

For general vulgarity and ghastliness, a German scoops the prize, though it is a close-run thing with Hearst (newspapers) and his appallingly frightful house, known to us, more or less, by its counterpart in Orson Welles' *Citizen Kane*.

Alfred Krupp (guns and death), determined to have an immense house where he could entertain the Kaiser, managed to construct a building which reminded everybody of Cologne railway staion. No wood was used (inflammable) and there was no gas (dangerous). None of the windows opened (draughts). Krupp's study was purposely situated over the stables: the ammoniac fumes from horse-dung were said to be A.1 for the lungs and were fed into the room through special ducts. Here Krupp invented ever bigger and dottier guns, one of which could fire in opposite directions (such a boon) at the same time. When he tired of that, he roamed the 300 rooms, pinning up grumpy little notices forbidding guests to do this or that. But then, one could expect anything from a man who, following a time-and-motion study, forced the workmen in his enormous factories to get *written* permission from the foreman to go to the lavatory.

What is rather pleasing is that, amid the dreadful waste and almost total lunacy, instances of stinginess are rare. It is true that Paul Getty had a pay-telephone installed for his guests' use, but on the whole the rich rich have splurged the stuff happily out, notably the Rothschilds and the Rockefellers.

Giving away money was one of Scottish Carnegie's principal relaxations, and he had a word to say on the subject. 'The man who dies rich, dies disgraced'. Oh well, most of us are safe, and getting safer every day.

ODD COUPLE

(*The Two* by Irving Wallace and Amy Wallace)

Nearly everything about them was weird. Their mother was called Nok and their father Ti-eye. Their own names were Chang and Eng and they were brothers, born in 1811 and joined at the base of the chest by an arm-like ligament six inches by eight. They shared a common navel. They reared ducks and taught one of them to lie down, quack for food and walk the tightrope.

In due course they married two sisters, offspring of a mother who tipped the scales, or broke them, at 36 stone. Between them, and literally at that, they produced 21 children and they were, of course, the Siamese Twins.

They faced their nightmare plight with great dignity. Living and exhibiting themselves in America at 50 cents a peep, they had, prior to their finding wives prepared to cope with what one must modestly call 'the difficulties', been pursued by a girl who, falling passionately in love with them, wanted to marry both, a convenient arrangement, some might think. Need one say that the Church, so resourceful in finding let and hindrance for almost anything that looks as though it might turn out to be jolly, pointed out that this would be instant bigamy, rating a heavy gaol sentence.

As *The Two* relates, an enterprising trader called Coffin brought them from Bangkok to America and thence to Europe and other profitable centres, where they met the Czar and were handed gifts by a Queen Victoria quite pop-eyed with astonishment. Fortunately the connecting tissue was fairly pliable, permitting them to walk more or less side by side. Learned medical men ceaselessly examined them, finding that the pubic hair of both divided neatly into the same grey and black sections. While carrying out circulatory experiments, they stuffed one of them with asparagus to see if its unmistakable presence would manifest itself later on in the other (it didn't apparently).

Both were intelligent and talented. They played the flute, learnt languages, read poetry (Pope was their favourite author) and fretted increasingly at their appalling situation, its awkwardness now increased by the fact that Chang had discovered what a pleasant drink whisky was and that, the more you took, the rosier everything seemed to become. A physical separation, the dream of them both, would however have been too risky and no surgeon was prepared to attempt it.

Their end was hideous. Chang had a stroke and, partially paralysed, was put to bed. Eng, who seems to have behaved very well, joined him, willy-nilly. Waking one morning, he found his twin lying dead beside him, was seized by violent convulsions and joined him within the hour.

The bodies were hastily whizzed off to an autopsy in Philadelphia where a Dr Pancoast got busy, his bizarre findings (the two livers were joined together in some rum and unexplained fashion) causing astounded whistles in the pages of the *Medical Times*. The curious will rejoice to learn that portions of the bodies, preserved in formalin, can still be viewed in Phily's Mutter Museum and their name is likely to live on for ever. It was a fame miserably bought.

WINDSOR AND NEWTON

(*Queen Victoria's Sketchbook* by Marina Warner)

Grouse and grumble as she might and so constantly did about her allegedly sad lot, Queen Victoria did have, for much of her life, two great solaces additional to her happy marriage and Albert's obviously indefatigable marital attentions. One of them was recently discovered to have been the theatre (three visits a week was quite normal). And now we find from Marina Warner that, from 1827 to 1890, she ceaselessly sketched, painted and etched.

It was already vaguely known that she dabbled in such things, but this is no dabbler at work and the results fill over fifty sketchbooks and albums. 'She has been until now', Miss Warner writes, 'an unknown example of a marvellous and extinct breed: the Victorian amateur watercolourist'.

At the age of eight, bi-weekly and hour-long painting lessons began, and continued for nine years, with Richard Westall, R.A. ('very gentlemanly and extremely punctual'), lessons which brought much happiness into that muted childhood: and, much later in life, Landseer was to lend a tutorial hand. The diarist Greville, often so prone to take a dreary view of things, thought the Princess 'a short, vulgar-looking child' and a self-portrait at the age of thirteen shows a serious and tight-lipped girl already under considerable strain.

Like many another adolescent, Victoria had her youthful crushes and, combining them with her love of ballet and opera, her sketchbooks explode with drawings and watercolours of her two heroines, the dancer Taglioni and the singer Grisi. And then along came the Crown and, with it and perhaps best of all, Lord Melbourne, who figures frequently, usually in colour, that fascinating and enigmatic man who disliked all birdsong save the cawing of rooks and who by then was so firmly entrenched in her affections that, at her Coronation, Victoria could put up with his munching sandwiches and swigging wine from off the altar in St Edward's chapel and whom she subsequently and lovingly painted struggling along with the Sword of State ('excessively heavy').

Melbourne, like many Victorian men, had whiskers and there is no doubt that, as a manly attribute, the Queen was all her life rather a one for whiskers, preferably blond. They bristle splendidly in her sketches of Count Walfstein and Prince Esterházy, while the exiled Duke of Brunswick looks like a villain in a melodrama. Albert filled the bill in this respect ('Quite charming . . . delicate moustachios and slight whiskers') and, later, Napoleon III's goatee merited an especially careful study in profile. The bearded Indian 'Munshi', her servant, rates an admiring portrait and there are a number of John Brown ('Johnnie' to her apparently). And oh the excitements of early married life. 'I went in and saw him shave, a great delight to me'. Whiskers again, you see.

It is in her quick little pen-and-ink studies that this royal artist is at her best. The rather formal set-pieces of Scottish lochs and glens, Swiss mountains, charades at Chatsworth (she could never manage either legs or feet), and the environs of Balmoral (painted, a morbid note adds, 'in 1862, the first year of my misery') are too heavy by half, though sometimes she gets it right — there is a pleasing view of Torquay from the royal yacht. But the early and inch-long likenesses of the ponies that she daily rode succeed excellently, as do the multitudinous ones of her growing family and especially those of the adored eldest girl, the Princess Royal (known as 'Pussy' at home) in her bath and taking her bottle. It is strange that the Queen painted Albert hardly at all, and only once in the bosom of his family. She was perhaps aware that her purely amateur powers, and beyond a certain point they progressed hardly at all, were inadequate to reproduce the one who to her eyes was such a paragon of masculine beauty.

Victoria was very skilful at catching a facial likeness, alarmingly so in two cases. By the age of nine the character of the future Edward VII was all too clear. He had started to refuse lessons from his tutor, and to spit and scowl, and although his mother disliked his knock-knees and his drooping Hanoverian nose, she dutifully got out her painting materials and, with gloomy relish, preserved for posterity little Bertie's appallingly sulky and disgruntled face.

Her quick pencil drawing of her grandson, William of Prussia, at about the age of four really sends a shiver down the spine. His grandmother recorded the fact that the other

. . . she dutifully got out her painting materials

children 'are rather afraid of him as he is so violent'. There he arrogantly stands. Clap those upturned moustaches on him and sit him on a horse and he is instantly recognisable as the Kaiser, the vain and determined architect of many of our present ills and who, when he won, was going to hang us all from lamp-posts.

BEVERIDGE REPORT

(*The Road to Shangri-La* by Ann Beveridge)

In Shangri-La, as you'll recall, nobody ever grew any older (except perhaps those who were so ill-advised as to sit through that musical film about the place) and the name is here borrowed to illustrate Ms Beveridge's '60,000-mile quest for the secrets of rejuvenation'. Popping selflessly off and in all directions — Mexico, New Jersey, Japan, Chile, Portland Place — on her fine mission, she speaks of a 'brilliant' American scientist whose view it is that some of us 'could almost certainly still be around to see the year 3001', a *pensée* which must surely win a prize for the world's most depressing concept.

But how to achieve longevity and spruce oneself up? Whither to lug one's flabs and bags and sags and bulges? 'Not all of us', says our thoughtful authoress, 'can jet round the world in pursuit of youth.' No indeedy, and not all of us would wish to, but here's a tip or two, just in case. It seems that if you care to go and live in the Caucasus, pick tea on a collective farm, eat broiled goat and swig pomegranate juice and not say anything nasty about the Soviet system, your chances of reaching a century are quite rosy. Or you can settle in a remote Himalayan valley and munch absolutely nothing but apricots, fresh or dried, in which case you'll do even better (120).

Human aid is to hand in the shape of Dr Ivan Popov who, in the Bahamas, will rejuvenate you by stuffing you with fertilised hens' eggs and by bombarding you with sea-water (what we used to call 'splashing' I suppose), while high in the Bavarian Alps we find Dr Wieldemann waving a hopeful syringe full of 'the Bogomoletz serum' which is said to have been tried out during attempts to rejuvenate Stalin, himself hardly an advertisement for Bogomoletz Products one would have thought (I rather wonder if gifted Bogomoletz outlived his patient).

It is not long, of course, before Barbara Cartland comes shimmering along ('Whisper it quietly, she is 77'), speaking up defiantly for a substance which 'contains Vitamin FF' (what on earth can that be composed of?) and which with her has achieved 'a general firmness of the abdomen', cheering news indeed.

There is also a helpful confection called Royal Jelly, which I took at first to be the pudding course at those Informal Lunches but which turns out to be a busy bee product, secreted by the workers for their Queen and simply A.1 for increasing buoyancy (and I should hope so too at, apparently, £45 an ounce).

A multi-billion dollar world industry copes with the sad, rich ninnies who spend their time transporting their wrinkles from one health resort to another, smearing on miracle creams and glumly staring at themselves in the glass. Ms Beveridge will have given them fresh ideas for peregrinations and a fresh significance to 'pack your bags'.

PLEASE BE SEATED

(*Voices out of the Air: Royal Christmas Broadcasts* introduced by Tom Fleming)

Those of us who are old enough to have heard the very first Royal Christmas Broadcast from Sandringham in 1932 will remember well what the BBC so rightly calls 'the sense of occasion' and the feeling that it was a regal blessing being conferred on those sufficiently prosperous to own a receiving set (by no means a common household object in those days). Indeed, so impressive was the event that, as the somewhat guttural tones rolled out the platitudes ('It may be that our future will lay upon us more than one stern test. Our past will have taught us how to meet it unshaken'), whole families rose to their feet and stood with bowed heads. One might, good heavens, have been either in church or in Japan.

There was some surprise and a certain uneasiness on finding that we possessed such a foreign-sounding King, surprise that is until the richly European background and parenthood were recalled. Edward VIII, possibly wishing to be as different in this as in everything else, sounded like an American trying to speak Cockney. The slightly foreign voice hung on a bit with George VI but has since disappeared completely, to be replaced by a marvellously clear and limpid speech entirely suited to the material it is required to pump forth, for the normal and chatty tones of everyday conversation are barred. A royal occasion is hardly the moment for an animated flow ('My dear, I can barely *wait* to get to Balmoral').

Earlier in 1932, the king and queen had visited Broadcasting House, recently constructed (Reith 'got them round' in fifty minutes), while, and practically at the same moment, Professor Piccard, who looked like everybody's idea of a slightly cracked scientist, was ascending nearly 10½ miles in a balloon, for one of the features of Tom Fleming's pleasant résumé of the royal Christmas talks is to list items of interest that were going on elsewhere in the same year, and Piccard's basket then loomed

154

large in the public imagination.

Thus, in 1939 and while George VI was making what is possibly the most warmly received broadcast of them all, the one about 'I said to the man who stood at the Gate of the Year', we are reminded that the Spanish Civil War was ending, our Phoney War was on, and that the *Royal Oak* had been disastrously sunk.

It is interesting to discover that the Monarchy did not at first take kindly to the idea of broadcasting and that it required ten years of postal wooing to coax George V to the microphone at Christmas (and even as a listener he refused to have an aerial on the Sandringham roof). To get him going, His Majesty preferred, instead of the customary red light signal, a tap on the shoulder when it was time to start, and he had to be warned not to rustle or crackle his script. How merry to learn that he sat down too heavily in the favourite wicker armchair from which he was to speak and went right through the seat. Those hoping for some rattling royal oath (imagine Henry VIII!) will be disappointed. 'God bless my soul!' seems to have sufficed.

In 1932 the public reaction was ecstatic, and the *Spectator*, commenting on the moment when the king cleared his throat, cheered all its readers by saying 'A King who coughs is a fellow human being'. The hour-long round-the-world Prologue to the affair was tastefully summed up by the dear old *Morning Post* as 'a family re-union on a scale terrene'. It was estimated that his voice reached twenty million people and 'Paris talked of nothing else' Mr Fleming loyally and enthusiastically states, an announcement that at least one reader who knows the French takes leave to doubt.

With every royal message that one is now able to live through again (and many of us have heard all of them), one sympathises increasingly with the crushing formality of their lives, and the alleged fondness for practical jokes in private becomes entirely understandable. Jokes and the unexpected pleased — Victoria used to let out a happy peal when anybody tumbled over and measured their length, and wasn't it Queen Alexandra who adored apple-pie beds, when the apple-pie and bed belonged to somebody else, and this despite the fact that beds in general were a tricky subject when considered in connection with her rather fidgety royal spouse. Foreign princes used to squirt each other with soda-water bottles and ride bicycles up and down the palace corridors ('We *shrieked!*'). In others this activity would be called 'letting off steam', a conception that seems a shade incongruous when applied to Victoria, formidable even in death.

Who, one wonders, writes the royal speeches. A Secretary? A Courtier? Some dusty don? There has been, down the years, a fine continuity of style, and what else could the matter contain but words that are reassuring, forward-looking, dedicated, hopeful for the future, and breathing a general and Christian belief in the goodness of mankind. And very nice too.

SHAPE OF THINGS TO COME

(*Our Future* by Dr Magnus Pyke)

Magnus Pyke has dipped, like Tennyson, 'into the future, far as human eye could see', which in the case of *Our Future* is fifty years, and quite enough too.

The whiskery Laureate certainly foresaw aeroplanes and bombs and the League of Nations, for what *that* was worth, but Dr Pyke is altogether more productive and tells us that in half a century the world population is likely, the dreaded Russkis behaving themselves, to have doubled and we may well be inhabiting large floating island cities (bags I the Mediterranean) and be living in pre-fabricated 'instant' homes put together in room units like a child's house of bricks and enlarged or diminished at will.

The inner walls will be a honeycomb of stiffened paper filled with woolly material and bound by thick cardboard, pipes and roofs will be of plastic (don't forget that solar panel) and an over-abundance of free time (surely the future's main problem) will encourage us all to go in for D.I.Y. in a big way and put plumbers and builders out of business — trades not primarily identified with speed and co-operation and so serve them right!

Body heat and the hot air outflow from the fridge will warm our fully insulated rooms, garbage compressors will squeeze suitable kitchen waste into combustible brickettes for the Kosi-glow stove, and in a power crisis a bicycle-powered electric generator will work the Telly ('Come on, Gran, it's *Crossroads* and your turn to pedal'), and a three-dimensional Telly at that with a life-size screen so that you can almost reach out and touch Delia Smith's toad-in-the-hole.

Those who wish to will be able to sleep on a hover-bed, cocooned in warm air, and get woken by a friendly robot, clanking about on its spring-loaded joints and programmed to bring you tea at 8 sharp and croak out a cheery greeting ('Good morning, dear').

Burglars and thieves will be no more, for our house doors and windows will, like sesame, only open to the vibrations from our own voices, impossible to counterfeit, and credit cards will make us an almost cashless society. Medical treatment will be on a D.I.Y. basis, advice being given by the doctor's speaking computer ('Kindly show me your tongue').

'Come on Gran . . .'

To acquire a newspaper, just tap out a number on your home computer. Then there is a four second whirring sound and, hey presto, a pristine and home-printed *Sunday Telegraph* shoots out of the slot. Or a properly programmed computer will be pleased to supply a composite newspaper formed from articles and news items that the computer thinks will amuse you and from anywhere in the world — the *Washington Post*, *Le Matin* and the *Observer*.

Various inventive gadgets will eventually do away entirely with the postal service. My goodness, it's worth hanging on just for that alone.

ARISE, SIR HENRY

(Henry Irving and the Victorian Theatre by Madeleine Bingham)

Henry Irving, whose brilliance led the then despised acting profession into glory and respectability and who, in 1895, was the first actor to be knighted, and by Queen Victoria at that, had his early difficulties. He had a weird, strutting walk and a weak voice with a faintly Cornish twang to it. His thin legs and gaunt looks (said to be like a neat bank clerk's with poetical leanings) were not at all to the taste of the time, which liked a hero to look like one. But here were a burning talent and a ruthless determination that nothing could quench, not even the dampening advice of the great actor, Phelps, to whom Irving gave an audition ('Have *nothing* to do with the theatre').

He climbed the ladder the hard way and wisely chose to play anything that came along — a bad fairy in pantomime, the demon in *Puss in Boots*, together with appearances in deplorable tear-jerkers such as *A Poor Girl's Temptation*. There was a piece called *Little Toddlekins*, which one is rather glad to have missed, and a merry farce, *My Wife's Dentist*. In ten years of touring, he played 588 parts.

And so, widely experienced, to the Lyceum Theatre in London, where he found immediate success and the valuable association, both on and off the stage, with the adored charmer, Ellen Terry, who didn't really enjoy acting but who, in a permanent muddle with her finances and her husbands, had to earn the money (£300 a week, when times were good).

Irving's first smash-hit was *The Bells*, a chilling melodrama set in a snow-covered Alsatian village with Irving as a murderer for ever haunted by the sound of his victim's sleigh bells, the flickering gas lamps adding enormously to the dramatic effect. Photographs exist of him in this famous role and frighten one yet.

But his sights were set on higher things than making flesh creep. His *Hamlet*, staged for a mere £100, was a triumph and even the moronic Prince of Wales allowed himself to be dragged to it (he said subsequently that the only thing worth looking at was Ophelia). But from then on the Lyceum Shakespearean productions — *Merchant of Venice*, *Macbeth*, *Othello* — became increasingly lavish and beautiful.

No expense was spared. In *Faust*, with Irving as Mephistopheles, the foils were electrically charged and excitingly gave off devilish sparks and flashes (one actor, forgetting his glove, leapt, sharply shocked, high into the air).

Irving clearly had some mesmeric quality and that pale, ivory face could hypnotise an audience into accepting him whatever he acted, even as a 43-year-old Romeo, though one old lady was heard to say that he was old enough to know better, and a caricature was published, simply labelled 'Rummy-o'.

Wildly generous and entertaining constantly, he took care to look, off the stage, like an actor, with long, flowing hair, broad-brimmed hats, lengthy strides and a dreamy far-away manner. Rising above an early and disastrous marriage, he had latterly a happy home life with a Mrs Aria, a Jewish lady whose husband had deeply shocked her by emerging from a Synagogue service saying 'I wonder what's won the Lincoln Handicap'.

There were a dazzlingly successful and profitable tour of America (total takings, £150,000, then a vast sum) and command performances at Windsor and Sandringham.

The last years brought sadness. The Lyceum scenery store at Southwark went up in flames. The London County Council, insisting on costly fire-risk structural alterations at the Lyceum, effectively closed its doors to him for ever. He revived *Richard III* and, possibly tipsy, fell down and damaged his legs.

Financially insolvent and suffering from angina, he died, this very great performer, as he would have doubtless wished, on his farewell tour at Bradford, where a packed house had, a few minutes before, risen to an outstanding performance in *Becket*. He rests in Westminster Abbey and, as a boy and at services in the Abbey, John Gielgud used to gaze in awe at the slab marking his grave.

NOTHING
CAN BE NICER

NOTHING CAN BE NICER

'Can anything in the world be nicer than a really nice girl?' asks Mrs Humphry ('Madge' of *Truth*) in her book *Manners for Women* (1897). In this, and the companion volume, *Manners for Men*, Mrs Humphry deals at length with social observances and

. . . or at Lord's (*Saumon à la Zingari*) . . .

problems ranging from the direction of the tilt of the soup-plate to the correct method of addressing a Duchess. She writes ostensibly for the upper middle classes, but we know as well as she that her books are really a Never Never Land peep for the servant-girl and shop-assistant, a glittering day-dream in which the poor and imaginative can picture themselves at the Ascot party (*Côtelettes à la Connaught*) or at Lord's (*Saumon à la Zingari*) or at the Derby ('comestibles prepared at home').

Mrs Humphry's present-day counterpart has to confine herself, such is the raciness of our times, to marital disasters and in less distinguished strata: 'Go back to him, dear. Buy a new hat, giggle at his jokes, be your old friendly self, the lovely girl of your courtship days. He will soon forget this other woman'. Not so Mrs Humphry. Everything with her is nice, though the bicycling vogue allows her to sound a warning note to wheel-women on the dangers of promiscuous acquaintanceship, and she also advises strongly against making friends when abroad, although 'this need not hinder the manner from being pleasant and the tone genial'.

Mrs Humphry pays much attention to the correct method of laughing. 'There is no greater ornament to conversation than the ripple of silvery notes that forms the perfect laugh.' The latter can be acquired, Miss Florence St John having learnt to laugh by singing a descending octave staccato with the syllables 'Ha ha!' Mrs Humphry speaks with admiration of a laugh heard at a theatre (from the stalls, naturally): 'a single silvery note of musical mirth . . . . It was but one note — say E flat on the treble clef'. Do not be dismayed if E flat is beyond your range: 'there is in London society a lady whose beautiful voice is generally admired. She laughs on two soft contralto notes'. 'Ha, ha' seems to be the sound to aim at, thus avoiding 'the shrill and attenuated "He! He!" and the double chuckle "Ho! Ho!"' not to speak of 'the coarse "Haw-haw" of the uneducated'. Mrs Humphry runs out of aspirated aitches when trying to describe 'the horrid, luscious laugh of the man who appreciates a nasty innuendo'. Laughter, E flat or otherwise, 'defeats the spleen' and its 'careful culture . . . should be attended to'.

With our laugh diligently practised, we are ready for the dinner-party but first let Mrs Humphry describe a table decoration of the period: the colour *motif* is pink.

Down the centre was a drift of rose-pink and silver gauze, in itself a delicious bit of colour and texture. It was bordered with long trails of smilax which passed under miniature arches of holly and mistletoe. In the centre of the table rose a small ivy tree, hung on all the branches with peals of tiny bells, which tinkled with fairy music at every movement of the guests. Trails of smilax hung from candelabra to candelabra, all down the table, tied with pink ribbon, and the candles were shaded with pink. The small vases at the corners were filled with pink roses and brown ivy . . . . Pink-shaded lamps and baskets of flowers, chiefly pink tulips . . . tied with pink ribbons . . . stood at points of vantage through the room.

Settle at the table and, first of all, consult 'the dainty little bill of fare' and make a mental note of any favourite dish 'so that it may not be refused'. Converse with your neighbour ('does she paint, has she read the novel of the hour, does she bike?') but do be careful: 'the viands must never be chosen as a topic . . . but if one knows a girl very well, one may ask, "Do you like sweets?"' The bewhiskered must be wary: 'it requires some expertise and practice for a man with a moustache to take soup in a perfectly inoffensive manner'. 'An occasional "Thanks" to the servant is not amiss . . . I have observed that when a neat and pretty parlourmaid waits at table she is more likely to be thanked than a manservant . . . I offer no explanation of why this should be so. I merely record the fact as I have noted it.' 'The mouth should be closed while mastication is going on', and remember that the skins of grapes 'have to be expelled as unobtrusively as possible. . . . The forefinger is curved above the mouth in a manner which serves to conceal the ejectment'.

In some matters of which she treats, the lead is given by the Royal Family, and Mrs Humphry appears to have been an accurate observer of the Court and of the Queen. 'When listening to addresses or long speeches, an expression of weariness, sometimes amounting to indifference and even apathy, occasionally settles down on the Royal countenance.' There is a splendid understatement in the sentence: 'the royal disapprobation of cosmetics, hair-dyes, and other forms of insincerity in personal appearance is not veiled in any way'. However, a droll mishap puts everybody in good spirits, and when a lady who caught her shoe in her skirt while curtseying had to be carried from the Presence Chamber there was much amusement, 'a broad smile appearing on the Queen's own face, while the young princesses tittered irrepressibly, and the Princess of Wales bit her pretty lips. The Prince looked as if he longed to give one of his great guffaws' ('Ha, ha' one hopes).

'The humble omnibus', says Mrs Humphry, 'may be thought by some readers too democratic a kind of conveyance to be considered in a book on manners. Not at all!'

> This vehicle used to be disdained by gentlewomen, but the wave of democracy that has of late swept over us has allowed us to perceive the utility of this among other cheap things. It may be a question if well-dressed women have really the right to occupy seats in these public vehicles to the frequent exclusion of the poorer sisters for whose convenience they were intended.

In certain respects, the wave of democracy has gone too far. 'At a theatre the underbred man is often in evidence, not only in the low-priced seats, but also all over the house. He has been seen — and heard — in private boxes.' And even in the omnibus Mrs Humphry considers that the underbred are too prone to brush against one and to have no 'delicate sense of self-respect'. How easy it is to tell who is who: 'though the fashionable manner inclines to a rather marked decisiveness and the fashionable voice to loudness, even harshness', these are immediately distinguishable from 'the lively gestures, the notice-attracting glance and the self-conscious air of the underbred'. Even gentlemen whom one thought that one could trust sometimes 'let themselves down to the frequenting of public-houses and places of amusement, where the entertainment has been carefully planned to suit the uneducated, the low-born'. Waves of democracy, it is clear, must be small, otherwise they disturb the pebbles and make a noise and nobody is safe from a splashing.

The proper display of emotion requires some guidance: 'so very fashionable and elegant is modern mourning that the lavish use of crape in its initial stages is an absolute necessity'. Crape, of course, 'is to announce to friends and acquaintances and others that our loss is so recent and our grief so acute that we must be excused from ordinary conversation'. There is, however, cheerful news for widows, black woollen gloves being no longer necessary, '*suèdes* and silk gloves are permitted and in a couple of months are succeeded by French kid'. Collars and cuffs of white batiste may also 'lighten the intensity of their weeds'. The acuteness of the grief is carefully measured, husbands getting crape for a year and black for a year, grand-mothers three months' crape and two months' black, aunts black for two months and modified black for one, and a cousin two months' black. Friends, one assumes, crape or black to taste.

Emotion at weddings must be equally strictly controlled. Although it used to be *de rigueur* in the vestry, and sometimes at the breakfast as well, 'crying is no longer fashionable. It has followed fainting into the moon-light land of half-forgotten things'. An emotional bride may, should she feel inclined, shed a furtive tear or two at parting from 'the dearest old dad in the world' or 'darling mums'.

Mrs Humphry spreads herself on weddings: invitation cards from Parkins and Gotto, patent boots for the bridegroom, brown or bay horses ('better taste' than grey); curb the servants, who are usually 'nearly wild with excitement', and on no account have too large a cake, Mrs Humphry having heard of one which, with a fine electroplate stand twenty-seven inches in diameter, succeeded in bringing down the table on which it rested together with the ceiling of the room beneath. Should the fireplaces in the reception-rooms be concealed 'beneath a wealth of snowy blossoms', heat can be supplied when necessary 'by means of two or three wrought-iron crates filled in with cathedral glass, enclosing asbestos heated by means of oil, a highly decorative mode of heating . . . But think', even

Mrs Humphry adds, 'of the cost of all this!'

Warnings are given where warnings are needed: don't wear white petticoats and black patent shoes on the river, don't take the umbrella into the drawing-room; don't wear thick walking-boots at a formal dinner-party; don't be *décolletée* at the casino; don't ride rapidly past invalids in bath-chairs; don't smell of tobacco (which may 'offend the olfactory nerves of women'); don't wear patent boots with a shooting suit; don't occupy more than eighteen inches of space in church; don't travel in bead trimmings and elaborate embroideries; don't reply 'both please' to a choice of Chartreuse or Benedictine.

Helpful as she is to both sexes, Mrs Humphry is perhaps at her best when dealing with girls and their 'cheery, breezy, young existence'. Freedom is in the air, indeed 'the girl of to-day hardly knows what Berlin wool-work means'. There is so much to be done. There is dancing ('. . . the fun of it, the go and whirl and mere merry motion'): there are the grand Balls ('May I have this barn-dance?') where one's ideal of manhood may appear, in the correct boots. If one's luck is really in, he will have wetted his hair, brushed and parted it, and then swathed his head with linen bands until it dries, thus producing 'the plastered appearance which is now recognized as good form'. There is curtseying to be practised ('Down you go, as far as the suppleness of your limbs will permit') and bicycling and rowing, and there is French to be learnt, as well as 'the gentle art of snubbing'. And everywhere there are young men to open doors for you, to give you flowers, to exercise 'well-bred self-control', and to hold umbrellas over you should the weather prove inclement.

The girl of to-day is, in fact, 'far too well occupied in enjoying herself — riding her bicycle, punting herself about on the river . . . and making sunshine in her home — to have much time for profitless self-analysis'. Exhaustive as her list is, there is evidently one 'Don't' that Mrs Humphry has omitted: 'Don't think'.

YET MORE
SUNDAY BEST

FOOD GLORIOUS FOOD!

Even a mind as richly stocked as the one I am privileged to possess usually manages, most days, to learn some new fact of interest and the information has only recently come my way that the late Mr Gladstone, preparing himself for slumber in No. 10, had his hot water bottle filled, not with hot water as in the ordinary way and hence the name, but with, as a variation, hot soup.

The alert brain instantly supplies two explanations for this somewhat eccentric behaviour. The first is that some distinguished scientist of the day — Faraday perhaps, or the young Rutherford — had assured the then Prime Minister that hot soup keeps hot for an appreciably longer period than hot water, particularly if a substantial *potage* is used rather than a thin *bouillon*.

The second explanation, and one which seems to me to be far the more likely, is that Mrs Gladstone suffered from what the advertisements used to call 'night starvation' and found it impossible to struggle through the wee small hours without having recourse to a few sustaining gulps of mulligatawny or a nutritious cockaleekie.

To alert the household at 3 a.m. with a wild cry for soup would have been an unpopular move, hence the bottle in the marital bed and, doubtless, her urgent call of 'William, I have severe hunger pangs. Quickly dear, unscrew your top'. In those days the bottle would of course have been one of those delightful stone ones which would not have impaired the delicate flavour of a *bisque de homard* or a Scotch broth. I like to think of her also reaching out for a handful of stale croutons from a jar labelled STALE CROUTONS.

Is it still remembered that Mr Gladstone's favourite pastime was the felling of trees (what a meal a psycho-analyst could make of this) and that once in an absent-minded mood and perhaps while pondering yet another witty retort for the House (an amusing play on the word 'seats' maybe!), he felled a tree in which one of his children was happily perched, munching an apple. No fatality occurred, I am glad to say, and a jovial 'ups-a-daisy' put all to rights.

I do not somehow see our present Leaderene, famous for keeping late hours, quaffing, as dawn breaks, a bedroom beakerette of rather rubbery Cream of Vegetable. I do not seem to see a hot water bottle coming into her scheme of things at all. She always looks warm as toast and I fancy her to be just a happy tingle-toes, luxuriating in her very own brand of central heating.

But what does Mrs Thatcher *eat*? I note that she continues, year after year, to entertain large numbers of guests to luncheons (a week or so ago the numbers attending one of her beanos amounted to surely a rather excessive 63, nice though it was to see that the out-of-fashion Callaghans were getting a free stoke-up) and one can only hope that she and her cook haven't moved with the times and gone in for that fearful *nouvelle cuisine* of which I have written and of which I give another alarming sample — 'Kipper fillets marinated in coconut milk, tenderly nestling in a noodle bed and excitingly topped with hot chocolate sauce dusted with parmesan'.

In these hard times need there really be quite so many guests to welcome, say, an obscure Eastern diplomat? Some years ago when Heath was at No. 10 and dispensing hospitality, smiles, music and flawed vowels, I spotted that he had invited to dinner over fifty male guests of the professorial kind and I wrote politely to ask (for after all I had, if indirectly, helped to fund the function) what the menu had been and what wines had gone gurgling down the red lanes. But answer came there none from poor chubby-chops and mum was the word.

In the highly improbable event of my ever being summoned as a guest to Downing Street, I intend to pretend to get into a muddle and to wander, not into No. 10 but, accidentally on purpose don't you know, into No. 11, the Chancellor's abode. Recent snaps of Mr Lawson, seen both head on and in ample silhouette, convince me that his cuisine is one in which one can repose complete confidence.

NAMING NAMES

Have you ever noticed that a book to which one has constantly to refer always tends to fall open at the same page? Thus, my desk dictionary (Chambers, natch, though for weighty matters my two-volume Webster is to hand) invariably supplies me with page 701, at the top and foot of which I find the word 'mulligrubs'.

The television game of which I am privileged to be a part requires three definitions, two of which are bluffs, of obscure words. What then of mulligrubs? Is it a Malaysian insect that attacks gum trees, or a primitive form of yeast used in Roman Britain for fermenting herbal wines, or a Victorian cockney term for contaminated food?

In point of fact it is none of these three possibilities but merely a word meaning a flatulent distension of the abdomen or, more generally, sulkiness. Is my dictionary, I wonder, trying to tell me something? However, the true definition represents An Escape. For what if centuries ago some writer had been rather taken with the sound of the word and had written a tale, Canterbury or otherwise, about a 'swete Mistresse Mulligrubs' and the name had then gradually come to mean 'woman'? And, down the years, from 'woman' to 'wife' is but a short step.

Picture the distasteful present day result. 'I was wondering if you and your mulligrubs could dine on Thursday.' 'I shall have to consult my mulligrubs.' 'Dost thou, Eustace, take thee, Mildred, to thy lawful wedded mulligrubs?'

'What's in a name?' cries Juliet in her night attire and risking a severe chill out on that Verona balcony, forgetful of the fact that behind her on the bedside table an unattractive skin is already forming on the surface of her bedtime mug of Slumbertight (Hot Malted Drinks Bring Forty Winks). She goes on, short of something to say I suppose (and why isn't she speaking

175

in Italian?), to inform us that if a rose were called something else it wouldn't matter in the very least.

My answer? Rubbish! For the really sensitive it would make a big difference. What if our word had never been 'rose' but we had, as usual, pinched a word from elsewhere? My knowledge of the Dutch language is sketchy, but suppose our word for rose had come from the Netherlands and we found ourselves landed with something like *Schtinkblume*, anglicised as 'stinkbloom'. What follows? 'My love is like a red red stinkbloom'. 'The last stinkbloom of summer'. 'Mighty lak' a stinkbloom'. In this last quotation, is a saucy wartime nightclub version still remembered?

> Sweetest li'l' feller,
> Everybody knows;
> Dunno what to call him,
> But I think he's one of those.

And now there comes surprising news about the Christian names bestowed at the font on young persons. The names may affect their examination results for two Mancunian psychologists, inspired by who knows what random suspicion, have discovered that the name Alison at the top of an English essay (What I Did In My Hols) is likely to get a rosier reception from an examiner than, say, the name Beryl. Similarly, it's jollier in this respect to be called Steven rather than Norman. The 'swing' between the likes and dislikes is said to be about 4%.

Whatever next! Will wretched parents have to bear the point in mind when deciding between Caroline and Cynthia? Whatever chance is there for Maud, Walter, Phoebe, Evangeline and Jabez? Will there be somewhere a chart showing examiners' preferences? And what about abbreviations? Will Len pack more of a punch than Leonard? Is Sid better than Sidney? Incidentally, for some time I thought there was an English Test cricketer called Chrissold and I fell to wondering what his Christian name might be.

The current craze for, in names, shedding syllables (Ben, Ron, Viv) from names or otherwise tampering with them would have had rum results some years ago — Alf Tennyson, Rudy Kipling and Wally Scott.

YOU'RE ENTITLED

Christmas is the time of year when the editors of newspapers and periodicals encourage their regular writers to name their favourite Books of the Year and a flood of titles, some remembered but the majority forgotten, burst excitingly upon the public. *Pick a Peck of Pepper*? Now what on earth was *that* about?

One's first reaction is dismay. What is the opposite of the description 'well read'? 'Ill read'? Whatever it is, one is it. But then the feeling of inadequacy is followed by one of relief that one had never clutched up and begun to read *The Great Awakening. A History of Abstract Thought in Latvia. Phase VIII: 1882–84.*

Nobody produces more satisfactory book titles than Barbara Cartland (*Love Rides Pillion* is a fine example) for ideally a title should give the reader some idea of what he is in for and Miss Cartland, bless her, always makes everything crystal clear. Elsewhere, *Crimson Her Chariot Wheels* can only be a graphic account of Queen Boadicea's more vigorous and successful campaigns, while *Paunch and His Judy* is obviously a light-hearted description of Napoleon's love life.

Sometimes titles have been chosen for their relative obscurity and who would ever guess *For This Relief, Much Thanks* is the biography of the Edwardian sanitary engineer responsible for a chain of greatly admired public lavatories in London's East End. If one may make a helpful suggestion, *Tomorrow and Tomorrow and Tomorrow* would do well for the autobiography of the excellent Mr Lett to whom so many of us turn at Christmastime for our diaries.

To those authors who experience difficulty in providing that absolutely right title for their cherished *oeuvre* I recommend a close study of *Hymns Ancient and Modern*. Here possibilities abound. 'The Trivial Round, The Common Task' (A survey of

Victorian House-Maids). 'Change and Decay in All Around I See' (Dentistry Down the Years). 'The Earth With Its Store of Wonders Untold' (A History of Harrods). 'Ten Thousand Times Ten Thousand' (Mathematics for Beginners).

All hymn-singing schoolboys know that 'One the earnest looking forward' refers to the captain of the school XV and Siegfried Sassoon got into terrible trouble as a boy at Marlborough for choosing for house prayers, for which he played the piano, Hymn No. 457. It is headed 'For a Holy Matron', verse 2 beginning 'Such holy love inflamed her breast' and the house Matron, who was present, considered herself to have been mocked and insulted. So do watch out.

And there is available another fruitful source of inspiration, with all risk of copyright payments over, the authors now being all presumed dead. Nobody could ever accuse the Old Testament of being a cheerful compilation and much of it is admirably suited to the provision of titles for the gloomier writer. Tent pegs are misused, boils burst, teeth gnash, bowels and loins either yearn or get girded up and everybody is quite tremendously grumpy almost all of the time. People find themselves being cursed right and left and all live to a vast old age to allow bags of time for them to get cursed in. Do get going. Ferret about for the title of your dreams. *Pillar of Salt* would do excellently for A History of Cerebos, and *Midhurst is my Washpot* is ideal for a grim working-class tale of the last century, set against a background of Sussex laundrymen. I am not quite clear what use to make of 'Daub it With Slime' (Moses and the bulrush ark) or 'Fire in his Bosom' (Proverbs), but that's now up to you.

There are many more splendidly suitable book titles than poor ones. If ever I were asked to award a prize for the best title ever, I would award it to Stella Gibbons. Has there ever been a title more absolutely, utterly right than *Cold Comfort Farm*?

OUT OF THE ARK

With our ever increasing knowledge of the effects of various foods and diets upon the human body and personality (even seventy years ago there was in the *Boy's Own Paper* a thoughtful article entitled FAT MAKES DUFFERS), one regrets more and more that writers and historians have provided down the years so very little information about the calorific and nutritional intake of their subjects.

For example, on the day after Duncan's little set-back in the Inverness Castle spare room, what did Lady Macbeth, a busy, caring hostess if ever there was one, tell the cook to prepare for lunch? It was hardly the moment for underdone beef and Macbeth's appetite may have been a trifle sluggish and in need of coaxing ('Come dear, another soused herring?'). But Malcolm and Donalbain, surprised to find themselves orphans, were nevertheless growing lads and certainly required feeding.

There should have been of course a number of left-overs from the evening before (the Macbeths seem merely to have picked at their food) and so I dare say that Mrs Mactavish acted on her own initiative, put the remains of the cold salmon through her processor, added cream and a pinch of nutmeg, adjusted her seasonings and produced quite a tasty mousse, followed by a rich salmi of venison (pity to waste it) with a turnip purée and a beetroot salad on the side. Any remains from the mousse would have done as sandwich fillers for Malcolm and Donalbain's saddle-bags. You'll recall that, for some piffling reason, they both became huffy, made off pretty sharply and didn't wait for the funeral. There's manners for you!

And what, may I ask, about the Elsinore *cuisine*? Not much calorie-counting there I'm afraid for Hamlet was fat and scant of breath (our informant was his mother, who knew a fatty when she saw one) and Gertrude herself was obviously a martyr to Danish pastries, wolfing them in batches in the intervals of misbehaving herself. And I've often wondered if Ophelia didn't go bathing too soon after lunch. I seem to see her tucking in to fried pork chops, mash, and banana custard and washing it all down with a beaker of the new Wondermalt milk shake, Flavoureen. Not easy even to float after all that. But you see, we don't *know* and so much has to be guesswork.

And now to another question but one to which answers may shortly be forthcoming. You will have seen a recent exciting announcement to the effect that an American team, valiantly scrabbling up Mount Ararat, came upon 'a boat shaped formation' at the surprising height of 5,000 feet, the 'formation' corresponding to the Ark measurements as given in Genesis. A large bag full of 'Ark samples' is to be whizzed away to the US for examination. And the question is, What did Noah and party eat in the Ark? With what was the galley stocked?

Have, one so wonders, any cooking utensils survived — a primitive primus perhaps, or a Kozibake mini-oven? Once the Ark was afloat one's sympathies go out to poor old Mrs Noah, rather a shadowy figure but struggling away to provide what must have been mainly vegetarian dishes. After all, if you are going to expect a ram and a ewe to produce, in course of time and after friendly overtures, sheep, it isn't sensible to let your thoughts dwell on boiled mutton and caper sauce. Noah was by then five hundred and ninety-nine years old and dentally can't have been up to much, but what of Shem, Ham (unfortunate name) and Japheth, lusty sons with good teeth and jumbo appetites? Quite a challenge to even a young cateress, let alone such a veteran as Mrs Noah (age not given but probably around 580).

What then was available in the way of tasty vegetarian foods? Here I am greatly helped by an erudite book that deals with the botany of the bible. Garlic was to hand and was doubtless freely used, its second-hand offensiveness being as nothing compared with the truly dreadful smells that must have been present. There were melons and millet and mint. There were leeks and lentils galore. There were beans and peas and members of the potato family. There may well have been pickled gherkins. I don't mind betting that Mrs Noah's *macédoine de légumes* was the talk of the state rooms.

One thing worries me. The only survivors of the Flood were the Noah family and, after the boat grounded on Ararat, there was at once a huge population explosion. But surely that must mean that they . . . . Oh well: never mind.

WHO'S A PRETTY BOY?

Some will already know my keen interest in those isolated historical facts that tell one so much and may perhaps recall my discovery a few years ago that the immensely rich Queen Victoria was stingy with lavatory paper and forced her Osborne House guests to make do with the neat squares cut from back numbers of 'The Thunderer', a rather unyielding material that would have needed some getting used to.

And now another unusual item has come my way, namely that Miss Radclyffe Hall had a parrot that had formerly belonged to George Robey, a very unlikely linking of names. Unless a parrot actually lays an egg and then goes and sits on it in a gritty corner, its sex remains for ever a mystery but this particular bird appears to have been presumed by its woman owner to be female and bore the rather fancy name of 'Karma'.

A word of explanation for younger readers. George (later Sir George) Robey was a famous music hall and revue comedian. He sported heavily accentuated half-moon eyebrows (they looked not unlike small Canary bananas that had gone bad), specialised in mild indecencies and was always billed as 'The Prime Minister of Mirth'. Mirth is not readily associated with Prime Ministers though genial Mr Heath, shoulders wildly shaking, did his chubby best, subsequent events revealing what a mistake it had all been.

Although Radclyffe Hall always sounds as though it must be a newly founded Oxford College for women, it was in fact the name of a novelist who in 1928 upset a number of people by writing and publishing a book called *The Well of Loneliness*. It is all about ladies who like other ladies quite a lot and to read now is about as sexually disturbing as an early Angela Brazil.

One's sympathetic old heart really goes out to that poor parrot. Most such birds have a seafaring background and are accustomed to robust jokes of a nautical kind and to the salty chat of jolly jack tars. Who can doubt that the Robey household suited 'Karma' to perfection, with Sir George playfully digging her in the ribs on his return from the theatre and regaling her with the very latest Stock Exchange joke ('There was this commercial traveller . . .').

To be transferred from such a wholesome, extrovert and healthy ambiance to the sadly strained and tense emotional surroundings cooked up by Miss (and how) Hall (she liked to be called 'John' — such a muddle for a bird) and her chum, Una, Lady Troubridge, would put a severe strain on a parrot, a strain almost amounting to cruelty. Sad that it is now far too late to call in the RSPCA.

Well then, I am far from happy about the genuineness of that name 'Karma'. It sounds to me as though Una, Lady Troubridge has been at work, tampering. It is not at all a name that would come naturally to a sailor and would clearly be considered very sissy in the 'fo'c'sle' (did you ever *see* so many apostrophes!). I don't mind betting that it was a male bird and was christened a hearty 'Bob' or 'Dick'. It would of course, and never underrate a parrot's intelligence, have instantly noted the change of name and sex and much resented it. 'Karma' indeed!

There is anyhow, when all is said and done, not much that is recommendable about a parrot's existence. It leads a very exposed life and the sanitary arrangements are laughably inadequate. At all times draughts blow. To effect a change of scene gymnastics are required. The food, though usually plentiful, is monotonous. Intelligent conversation is lacking, the constant repetition of 'Who's a pretty boy then?' being merely insulting.

But I did once see a bird that had struck it rich and was destined for great things. In the Pet Department of a well known Knightsbridge store it was their custom, after the purchase of an inmate, to label cage or basket, awaiting removal, with the name of the purchaser and thus it was that for a happy month a most distinguished and self-possessed parrot faced the world, and how very proudly, as 'Sir John Gielgud'. It was clearly well up in theatrical matters and knew the very best when it saw it.

NO MOD CONS

At my age it is not easy to understand and absorb new words and when I first heard 'aggro' I got the wrong end of the stick.

The first syllable, 'ag', I naturally took to be shortened form of 'agriculture' (cf Min of Ag. and Fish.), and the second syllable, 'gro', I assumed to be a lightly abbreviated 'grow', and I came to the conclusion that the word itself must therefore be a new form of chemical fertiliser. For many months I looked keenly about me for advertisements saying THIS YEAR WHY NOT PAMPER YOUR ROOT CROPS WITH AGGRO THE SOIL ENRICHMENT THAT HAS IT ALL.

And the same sort of bewilderment descended on me when I first heard working persons loudly complaining that their differentials were being eroded. What were differentials and, if I myself unwittingly had any, where were they? I vaguely pictured them in a deed box and the kindly Manager of the National Westminster himself mounting guard over them and preventing erosion.

I've never been much good at technical terms either. When, long ago, a mechanic peered under my bonnet and said 'You've blown a gasket', I staggered back in alarm, clutched the Sunbeam's tonneau hood for support and tried to remember my doctor's telephone number.

When, in the first house I ever owned (it will also be the last as I intend to leave it feet first) I required some alterations made and called in builders and plumbers and electricians, technical terms were everywhere. 'You do realise, don't you', somebody said, 'that your overflows must have Nuisance Value?' 'But *of course*,' I replied, totally at sea, but I was eventually able to discover that it meant that if there were to be a malfunction in my cistern's ball-cock (what *is* that doctor's number?), the splashy result must be visible to all. Well, a number of things in my life have possessed Nuisance Value (teeth, taxes, Hitler) and

I can easily manage one or two more. There are now no fewer than three overflows but they seldom commit a nuisance (Penalty, £5).

Then the lawyers weighed in with some of their highly specialised jargon and asked me, after the house was bought, whether it had a satisfactory 'title'. At first I understood this to be a hint that I should change the house's humble name to Chatsworth, possibly, or Blenheim. But here 'title' seems to mean solid proof of ownership or some such. I would have thought that handsome amounts of cash shelled out would be as solid a proof as anybody was likely to need.

When central heating was being considered, the word 'rad'

'You've blown a gasket'

185

was much bandied about. 'This'll have to be a three rad room,' and so on, 'rad' being plumbers' chummy talk for 'radiator', but the walls, mainly of stone and three feet thick, ruled out rads.

I don't go in much for electrically-operated kitchen appliances as here a modicum of co-operation from the user is required and the numerous Warnings, printed in red, baffle and fuss me. 'ON NO ACCOUNT switch on until your laminated swivel-bar is firmly locked into the grooved aperture (F on your chart)'. And that is not all. 'Beneath your flange-pin you will find a wee wart-shaped protuberance. Engage it carefully in the socket on your chamfered plate and CLICK, HEY PRESTO, your patented WHIRLYKRUNCH whirrs into action!'

However, if you don't mind radless rooms, hand-whisked eggs, not a sign of differentials, and the risk of being liberally splashed on from a height, do feel free to drop by for lunch.

OPEN WIDE

Some time ago, a *New Yorker* cartoon showed a dentist's surgery, complete with instruments of dental torture of which even the Elizabethans, years ahead of everybody else in ingenuity and proud indeed of their iron maidens and racks and thumb-screws, would have been envious. Two people were present — the horrified victim in the chair and the dentist, a deaf dentist as it happens who, just about to get alarmingly to work, was seen switching off his hearing-aid in order not to be able to hear the yells of pain and the screams for mercy.

My feelings about teeth and those who cope with this rather unlovely side of the medical art have been considerably modified by a newspaper article that recently came my way. 'Patients resent dentists and dentists resent patients' it says, starting strongly, but before you nod in vigorous agreement, spare a kind thought for those who prod and probe. Dentists, it seems, find their work not only physically tiring, which one expects, but also 'emotionally draining', which is news indeed. This explains at last those moments when they straighten up, down tools, leave the chair, dart behind a screen and make splashing sounds. I had always assumed that they were washing their hands or something, but now a great light has dawned. Quite drained emotionally, they are blubbing, and one's heart goes out to them in their distress.

Our splendid spokeswoman in all this is Miss Diana Knight, a dental adviser, and herself a practitioner, to the Patients' Association and a lady who plainly knows what's what. 'Dentists are human', she tells us, 'and they dislike being disliked. Subconsciously they feel the unfairness of it all . . .' and so in future, I personally am going, between their mutterings of 'this may hurt a little' and 'rinse, please', to let out loud cries of admiration and gratitude.

Miss Knight has got all the right ideas — make dentists'

rooms more colourful, she advises, and conceal the dental instruments as much as possible (even when produced, why not introduce guessing games to promote a relaxed atmosphere: 'I spy with my little eye something beginning with D'). Let the dentist greet you on neutral ground, it says, with a cheery 'Hullo there' in the reception area while you drink in the bright and saucy new clothes that he is wearing (those white coats do look as though major surgery is being contemplated). Let, in fact, Dentistry Be Fun.

The article then leaves teeth and moves on into the wider world of medicine and here again novelty is the thing. Medical skill is no longer, I read, considered to be enough by itself. Too one-sided. There is a great need to spread understanding about health and disease throughout the country's family doctor practices, so that when the shirt or blouse is opened and the chest tapped, both tapper and tappee know why.

This spreading of knowledge is to be achieved through the National Association of Patient Participation. Here I am on firm ground. If there is one thing that life has taught me in postwar Britain, with its parrot-cry of 'You'll have to wait three weeks' from anybody required to mend something or adjust something or supply something, it is how to be patient.

So I foresee a patient, leisurely stroll to the village hall to participate in Dr Boddington's lecture, illustrated with coloured slides, on 'Boils I Have Known' (next week: 'Your Spleen In Fair Weather and In Foul'). Then home, without hurry or bustle and, if one's luck is in, a repeat performance on radio or telly of *Dr Finlay's Casebook* with dear old Janet fussing away at mealtimes over her preoccupied medical charges ('Och, doctor, you've no touched me tatties').

It has been pointed out to me, however, that 'patient' here may really mean 'sick person'. Here a line must be drawn. What do they mean by participation? How far is it to go? If, for example, my leg has to be removed, I want, so to speak, no part of it. I am prepared to supply the leg, but there my participation ends. For the rest, let me be wafted away to dreamland while they get busy sawing.

WAKE UP

Bookworms and devoted readers the country over will have been much startled by a recent newspaper heading which said £20 FINE FOR DOZING IN THE LIBRARY. A new county by-law is aimed at discouraging persons who 'after a warning by a library officer, persist in sleeping'. Nobody, it adds, 'minds someone nodding off for a minute or two', and I should hope not.

To people who, like myself, have always relied on literature and club libraries to provide them with a really solid afternoon's sleep, this harsh by-law and fine come as a swingeing body blow, striking at our very roots. 'A bombshell' is not putting it too highly.

Everything in libraries is conducive to slumber, not least the books. There are the SILENCE notices, the steady breathing, the discreetly garbed lady librarian gliding about on flat soles, the occasional gentle rustle of a turning page, the warmth and the peace and the quiet and, of course, the dusty volumes themselves, literary treasures of a bygone age, such as *With Harrison to Jubbulpore* by Colonel W. J. Harty-McGurk and *To Tune My Lyre*, the collected poesy of Felicity Loynes, the 'Sweet Songbird of Staines' — the very book titles are a lullaby in themselves.

The library of my London club, dimly lit and looking out onto a quiet expanse of lawn, tree and shrub, is draped throughout the day and evening with slumbering members. Here we do not go in for a mere 'nodding off'. With us it is the real thing, the full z-z-z-z-z, each sleeper providing, as in a great orchestra, his own particular contribution — here the resonant timbre of a 'cello, there the tuneful flutings of the wood-wind or the explosion of a giant tuba — a vast melding of joyous sound and in open defiance of our SILENCE notice.

And, taking the wider view, I have always assumed that the

major part of our great English literary heritage was especially intended to bring healthful sleep with it. I am somebody, surely one of many, who has been able to achieve really deep and satisfactory slumber while the works of Shakespeare were being performed.

I do not mean during those rather noisy sections when, for example, the Macbeths are entertaining a house guest (such a fine host and hostess. What about those dinner parties!) or when poor old cracked King Lear has decided, and what a mistake, to go out for a stroll in inclement weather. I am here referring to those moments when a varlet, entering from the right and in a comical make-up, says to a varlet entering from the left, 'How now, sirrah? A pox on thee for a saucy knave!' and you know that it's going to be Fun Time in old Avon. Then I go out like a light, just coming to for the play's end, when the clown or the Duke or somebody advances solemnly to the footlights and says, in almost comprehensible lines, something which goes

> Thus one from each, and each from one and all,
> We liberate you from our story's thrall.

When you hear something rhyming in Shakespeare it is Cheer Up Time for it often signals the end of a scene, or act, or even the play.

One of my friends, many of them splendid theatre snoozers, I had not seen for some time but, going to a not very good imported American play (it was like a horse: exciting at both ends but dull in the middle), I heard his unmistakably melodious chest notes, increasing in volume, from the centre of the stalls, before he awoke, refreshed, for the interval and we could enjoy a good chin-wag.

But how on earth will 'library officers' apply this by-law? Will they go round gently prodding and separating nodders from genuine somnivolents? Will they be issued with a decibel-ometer, or whatever? Some people (and one must face these facts, however disagreeable) tend while they sleep to dribble. Will there be a dribbleometer?

The county involved in this by-law is Berkshire. At the very first opportunity I shall make a bee line for the Reading Public Library, settle down in a chair and drop off (to sleep, I mean, but perhaps both). Do join me. It will be well worth four crisp fivers to discover what happens.

LET ME TELL YOU

It has always been a pleasure to me to be able to pass on to the reading public a piece of really interesting, even sensational, information and I do so gladly whenever opportunity offers.

It may be recalled that quite recently I was in a position to tell you that all too little known fact that Angela Brazil was allergic to Christmas pudding (a grateful reader wrote to ask how she was with mince pies and I'm working on it). And although in the case of another famous lady writer I start to twitch nervously at the mere mention of her name, have you ever fully realised that Virginia Woolf used to buy all her hats in the palatial Oxford Street premises of Messrs Bourne and Hollingsworth?

Ready for more? Here goes then. Mary Baker Eddy had no fewer than three husbands and the middle one was, and how conveniently, a dentist. Did you ever! And Delius composed his first song in boyhood days and in the sanatorium of the International College at Isleworth after being concussed with a blow from a cricket stump during the school rebellion of 1879.

And now, in the strange way that things happen, life has caught up with me for, about six years ago, I passed on a fascinating statistic to the effect that there was actually sufficient ground space for the entire population of the world to stand, if with not much leg room, upon the Isle of Wight.

In addition I painted a startling word picture of the resultant chaos — all food shops drained of Hastyburgers, buses jammed to the doors, not a single raspberry yoghurt anywhere available and a mile-long queue for the Cowes GENTS. Just imagine the linguistic confusion (whatever can the Japanese be for COMMIT NO NUISANCE?). Furthermore, I stated the obvious fact that the weight of the world population would undoubtedly cause the Isle of Wight to sink beneath the Solent and be seen no more.

And this, I now learn, is precisely what is going to happen eventually (don't panic: there's bags of time to pack up and cancel milk and papers). An Isle of Wight geologist has announced that the island is, and I am sorry to say it, composed of inferior and non-water-resistant material and is being, year by year, reduced in size. He gives it about another thousand years, after which little will remain and most will have vanished.

Although Classical scholars will be thrilled by the thought of Freshwater and Ryde forming part of another Atlantis, the mythical underwater island which tempted the fertile pens of Pliny and Plato, all this submerging is pretty rough luck on the residents and I rather doubt whether her connection with Pliny is going to mean much to, say, a Ventnor landlady who has just splashed out regardless on a 'Whizzo' spin-dryer and a new Kumfysquat ('They're adjustable!') Toilet Seat.

Islands which come and go are still quite a novelty. There was certainly that volcanic one that, proudly steaming, suddenly heaved itself into view somewhere or other and is presumably still cooling down and making little burping noises as it settles. But on the whole islands tend to stay put, in particular and during the First World War, horrid little Heligoland whence came all those Zeppelins with what was then called their 'rain of terror' and which turned out to be a small selection of 25-lb bombs tastefully hand-dropped ('Open the window, Heinrich') from the gondola.

What about a final fact just to round off this feast of information? Dorothy Parker, who made so many laugh during her lifetime, wished to continue to do so after her death and she wanted a notice to be put on the headstone of her grave, a notice in such tiny letters that people had to crane forward and step on her grave in order to read it. And the notice just said IF YOU CAN READ THIS IT MEANS YOU'RE STANDING TOO DAMN CLOSE.

MUSIC HAS CHARMS

The eccentricities of the extremely rich make a fascinating study for the really well-heeled of this world all seem to share the same weakness — a sudden and unreasoning panic that they are about to become bankrupt.

A very rich family of my acquaintance feeling this panic upon them, decided on a programme of the strictest economy. It consisted of cancelling their subscription to *Country Life*. After a month, however, they found that existence without *Country Life* was intolerable and they re-ordered this admirable magazine, together with the four back numbers that they had missed.

The Dutch royal family is famous for, among other things, being rich, a fact which doubtless eased Queen Wilhelmina's declining years. Her special eccentricity was not a panic dread of poverty but a passion for that catchy number called 'The Teddy-Bears' Picnic'. I gather, and my informant is a most distinguished Oxonian writer and historian (the one that isn't A. J. P. Taylor), that at dawn a military band struck up this jolly, jiggy tune on the terrace below the royal bedroom, the melody being later entrusted, as the day wore on, to a pianist, a string ensemble, a harmonium, a jazz band and a full symphony orchestra. Even momentary silence and absence of teddies produced regal frowns and pouts and sulks and shrieks so that the tune had to be hastily repeated for the ninety-fifth time that day.

There is, heaven knows, nothing new about being soothed or stimulated by music. Those who commuted to London during the war will recall that the principal railway stations were flooded with assorted musical sounds — hurry music in the mornings ('The Flight of the Bumble Bee' and 'The Entry of the Gladiators'), with calmer stuff (the 'Indian Love Lyrics') for the late afternoon to ensure that a commuter would return home in a mood of quiet acceptance ('By Jove, dear, those whale steaks look tasty'). It is generally agreed that Waterloo's musical choice was tops, with Paddington a worthy second.

Since those pioneering days one has had to become accustomed, however reluctantly, to being bombarded in shops by those repetitive and tuneless idiocies called 'Pop' and now I note, with interest strongly tinged with dismay, a further musical encroachment and in, of all sacred areas, a bank. And not just any old bank, but my bank.

I felt sure, when the National Westminster authorities erected the tallest bank building in the City of London, that something was afoot in the way of daring novelty and now, lo and behold, here it is — an official announcement that branches in Wimbledon, Liverpool and Dorking have had music systems installed 'in their public banking areas, to provide their customers with pleasant ambience'. They add defiantly the highly debatable opinion that 'background music has a valuable contribution to make to the banking services'. They are particularly boastful about the Dorking branch where 'the Micro X system is situated in the first floor customer enquiry area, which creates a relaxed atmosphere but does not intrude into private discussions between the customer and bank staff'.

Although strongly disapproving of the whole thing, I am of course ready, in my helpful and courteous way, with musical suggestions for the Dorking manager. It is vital to strike a cheery note from the start so how about a joyous Wagnerian blast of 'Hail, Bright Abode' (sometimes translated as 'Dear Hall of Song') from *Tannhäuser*? And, to get you up the stairs to the first floor enquiry area, 'Colonel Bogey' would answer well. Customers wishing to swop banks might well be discouraged with a snatch or two of 'Abide With Me'.

Part of a manager's job is a sad refusal to grant overdrafts and here the musical sequence might be the 'Hesitation Waltz', 'They Didn't Believe Me' and the Dead March from *Saul*, rounded off with the merry 'Good-bye-ee' (the lyric continues with 'Don't sigh-ee, Wipe the tear, Baby dear, from your eye-ee').

There is, as you see, lots of room for musical enterprise and variation but all the same, as soon as music reaches my Devon branch, I'm ready with my ear-plugs.

NOTHING NEW UNDER THE GRILL

The London club of which I am proud to be a member, even though its founding fathers held political views that are not mine, has long been renowned, and rightly so, for the excellence of its kitchens. From 7 p.m. onwards the steady grind of molar on molar, the chewing and the champing, the munching and crunching and the 'Might I trouble you for the pepper mill', bear witness to the fact that that excellence is with us yet.

But I see to my dismay that the club has taken colour from almost every restaurant and hotel in the land and that a displeasing and superfluous verbosity has crept into the wording of its menus. It doesn't need Gertrude Stein to remind us that a pork chop is a pork chop is a pork chop, but no modern restaurant would allow it to get away with a description as simple as that.

Nowadays the kind of thing that you are likely to find in a menu is 'Baby lamb cutlets, pinkly innocent, tenderly tenderized in a gas-fired gas oven and waiting, a boon to dentures, on a fragrant bed of fennel and carraway seed, topped by butter-tossed courgettes!' Care to try to identify the following nutriment? 'Herb-strewn cylinders of selected pork meats daintily fried and with their juicy succulence then held captive in a delicate *choux* envelope'. Got it? But of course. Sausage rolls.

The humblest starter now gets the full treatment. 'Ripe, hand-picked and invitingly dark green avocado pear, neatly bisected and carefully de-stoned by an experienced avocado-chef, its creamy flesh laved in a spicy vinaigrette and cradled, awaiting your pleasure, on a shining Minton *assiette*'. And with fish we can really let ourselves go: 'A *tranche* of lordly turbot, pampered and gently steamed in a steamer and resting its magnificence on a macédoine of carrot, basil, marjoram and broken biscuit, flanked by decorative and taste-bud-teasing *blocs* (lumps) of vinegar-soused raw beetroot'.

Can all this twaddle be what seems now to be called *nouvelle cuisine*? Let me tell whoever invented *nouvelle cuisine* that there is nothing remotely *nouveau* about any of the main *cuisine* ingredients. How could there be? A turbot is a turbot and what's so new about that? What is *nouveau* is all this pretentious jazzing up and the phoney prattle that accompanies it.

' 'Ere be thy load, Jimboy'

In point of fact the rot set in some years ago and I lay the blame fairly and squarely at the engine-shed doors of British Rail. Travelling to Bournemouth in about 1962 and partaking of breakfast in the tastefully appointed dining car (soon of course to be abandoned in favour of Waitress Service plastic 'Kollapsilap' trays brought to your seat), I found on the menu not only 'oven-baked rolls' (where else could they be baked?) but also, to my total astonishment, an item described as 'dawn-gathered melon'.

And at once there sprang to my startled eyes a picture of the melon hothouses of Swindon and elsewhere and, as dawn broke, train after train stopping and the restaurant super-intendent alighting to gather up his supply of the sweetly scented fruit, lovingly tended by gnarled old gardeners all speaking in a gnarled old manner (' 'Ere be thy load, Jimboy'). When I asked the waiter what exactly was the meaning of 'Dawn-gathered', he replied that he thought it must mean that the melons had been gathered at dawn. I bit back the merry quip that I had prepared and just said 'Oh I *see*'.

For some weeks now, hotels have been busily advertising Special Christmas Turkey Dinners and I feel sure that not for a single moment will the happy diners be treated to just the bare word 'Turkey', or even 'Roast Turkey', on the menu. It's plainly too good a chance to miss. 'Blindfolded and then humanely-killed turkey, skilfully plucked by caring hands and stuffed with humanely-peeled chestnuts, oven-roasted till crispy-cooked and moisturised with its very own juices, nestling in a conglomeration of *saucissons*, with an accompanying relish of cranberry sauce fashioned from hand-culled berries.'

Why not have a go yourself? Plum pudding offers immense possibilities but to make bread sauce sound *nouveau* is something of a challenge: 'Hand-grated crumblets of the staff of life plunged headlong into an onion-infused beakerette of . . .'

MADE PUBLIC

I note that the BBC, ever mindful of what is brightest and best in the world of education, has trundled its telly cameras (with permission) into the hitherto sacred areas of a public school, Westminster in this case, and that 'a major new documentary' is promised.

Following the full and recent TV exposures (if that isn't in this instance an unfortunate word) of comprehensive schools, it was felt that public schools had been missing out and that a day by day peep at classrooms, dormitories, staff meetings, traditional ceremonies and so forth would correct the balance. Well, we shall see what we shall see.

Those of us with rich memories of this or that public school will be hoping that various prominent features of school life have not been overlooked. Athletics, for example, an event timed at most schools to coincide with the chilliest of March winds and the final snowfalls of the winter. Athletics enabled anybody who bore a grudge, justified or not, against his school to give rein to it on leaving by the sadistic gift of a silver athletics Cup.

No school has ever been known to refuse a silver Cup. Cups were competed for and promoted keenness. The Cup was always known by the donor's name and thus it was that trophies such as the Rumbold Cup for Junior Cross Country Running came into existence and ensured, year after year, an afternoon of total misery for some fifty junior boys, forced to stumble over ploughed fields, vault gates and get entangled in thorn hedges in a spirited attempt at a short cut ('Get back in the race, you filthy little rotter').

And here I should, incidentally, like to put forward a small claim. I and some of my fellow athletes, made to 'run for the Rumbold' and not greatly caring for rapid movement, used to progress at such a sedate and dignified pace, wobbling up and down quite a lot, that I may well have been, all unconsciously, the inventor of jogging, that modish and potentially lethal pastime. I just, in my modest way, mention it. Make of it what you will, for I have no further athletic claims.

Well then, I very much hope that we are going to see a member of the royal family opening something ('Three cheers for Princess Margaret') and tugging away at those little curtains that rattle back, or not, to reveal a commemorative plaque. Here again generous benefactors live on by name and the building to be opened is always something like 'the Morrison Gymnasium' or 'the Duckworth Laboratory'. When I was a schoolmaster, I used to think, irreverently, how jolly it would be if a royal would come down and close something instead. Schools always had plenty of ancient buildings ripe for closure. How novel and agreeable that would sound — 'It gives me much pleasure to close the Bagshaw Music Rooms', followed by a door firmly clanging to, the rumble of an approaching bulldozer and the first joyous crash of falling masonry.

I trust that there it not going to be too much mention made of modern comforts. Comfort was always suspect. Roughly speaking, the more uncomfortable the school, the better the education and the higher the fees. If bathrooms are to be shown, let it be made clear that the water in the taps is, at the best, tepid. School authorities in my day used to get very agitated about hot water. Cold baths were manly, but hot baths, with their hint of an almost Roman laxity and of an imperial decline, were dangerous stuff. Like beds that were too soft and 'gave' beneath one, nobody knew what excesses hot water might not lead on to.

A trip round the older buildings is always an eye-opener as almost everything at public schools used to be something else. 'You are now', the guide explains, 'in what was once the school laundry — Togger to so many of us — but which is now Matron's surgery and "den". The original bathroom or Tosher, is now the Computer Centre.' I hope, by the way, that we are going to see Matron herself in full operation, dealing briskly with suspected skrimshankers ('I've had enough of your rubbish') and with a defiant medical answer to each and every ill (cascara).

Goodness me, there's a lot of ground to cover. What of fagging and corporal punishment (the sound of a few hearty whacks and shrieks 'off', noises that are so much in the past spirit of these places, would remove any suspicion that privileged persons are being molly-coddled)? What about the school governors, good old Sir Something this and dear old Brigadier-General that? It is my view that no useful purpose is ever served by exposing school governors to public scrutiny and assessment.

Then, are the school menus and culinary arrangements going to be closely examined (I gather that all schoolboys now faint dead away if they have to go longer than 12 hours without fish fingers)? The school play presents problem after problem. Is it *all right* for Eyebright to appear as Ophelia or would it be wiser to play for safety and give this exacting role to the rugger captain?

What a telly scoop it would be if the 'roving camera' could manage to catch the headmaster fast asleep in Chapel or focus on a boy in the very act of trying to run away! Better still, what about a *master* trying to run away? Exciting visual possibilities abound. If the BBC wants help, it knows where to come to.

NAME THIS CHILD

Every year kind and informative people who evidently have time on their hands supply, culled from the few newspapers that still boast Birth columns, lists of the most popular Christian names bestowed during the year on newly born children, with James scoring heavily for the boys and Elizabeth ditto for the girls.

Sometimes parents allude to previous fairly happy events and one can sense the gritted teeth and stiff upper lips behind 'a sister for Jane, Anne, Jill, Ruth and Samantha' or 'the gift of a brother for John, Julian, Giles, Mark and Benjamin'.

The percentage of babies that get their arrivals announced in a newspaper is of course extremely small and the class of society from which the popular names are reported is a very limited one, for where in the lists are the Marlenes, the Tracys, the Deans, the Jasons and the Cindy-Lous? Modest suburban and village fonts would have a very different tale to tell, fonts where Osbert, Aloysius, Cuthbert and, forgive me, Peregrine would raise a priestly eyebrow and cause considerable consternation among godparents.

Various currently unpopular names bring back happy memories from the past for who would 'Clara' be but Clara Butt, the superb and statuesque contralto whose splendidly vibrant tones, especially in 'Land of Hope and Glory', rattled the Albert Hall walls and were said actually to have caused structural damage. Of considerable size as she was, her surname, preceded in one's mind by the word 'water', was perhaps unfortunate. In the very unlikely event of my being invited to make a return visit to 'Desert Island Discs' I would certainly ask for Dame Clara's famous encore number called 'A Fairy Went A-Marketing' and which found her in roguish and pixie mood, archly wagging a finger and fluttering her lashes. It was as surprising as if a chubby hippo had suddenly got up on its points and gone into Aurora's celebrated solo dance from Act III of *Sleeping Beauty*.

Another name no longer in vogue is Maud, made known to all in Tennyson's poem, the name providing a wealth of useful rhymes (best to overlook 'bored') and its familiarity making it a handy four-letter word clue ('She came in the garden') in crosswords. And 'Mona' is sadly now a rarity since the days when Itma's Mona Lott did so much to cheer wartime spirits.

Few things are stranger in America than the way they take the oddest names on the chin. Try these for size. Christian names — Sugarporn, Toilet, Chlorine, Phalla and Arson. Surnames — Turnip-seed, Chuckass, Boonjug, Ovary, Clapsaddle and Wack Wack. During the war I had as an agreeable colleague in SHAEF an officer called Milton W. Buffington III and every morning I had to attempt to get 'Hi, Milt!' to come trippingly off a tongue that normally made do with a courteous 'Good morning', accompanied by a cheery nod.

There are many once commonplace names that I miss — Cynthia (provided it doesn't get itself shortened to Cyn), Millicent, Thelma (apparently an invention eighty years ago of the writer, Marie Corelli), Sybil (shades of that beloved Dame), Tabitha, Nathaniel, Hubert and Grace, whether amazing or just ordinary.

The names used by Sapper in his stories make a fascinating study, blending as they do the improbable with the possible — John Manley, Carlton Bellairs (an actor, natch), Sylvaine Lankester, Mona Tremayne, Hilda Garling and Molly Venables. Bulldog Drummond's wife-to-be, Phyllis Benton, only daughter of a tipsy forger, is referred to as a 'topping filly', is described as being 'perfectly shod', can run very fast indeed and on this evidence it seems clear that she was, in point of fact, a horse. Drummond wouldn't have noticed, having other matters to occupy a mind not over-loaded with brain — cobras, acid baths, gorillas and notorious stranglers anxious to add another neck to their haul.

In the lists of names provided and covering the last three years, there are two surprising omissions, one boy and one girl. One is the name Peter, a reputable and euphonious name if ever there was one and I look to intending parents to put this right in future.

The other is the name Margaret. Yes, yes, I know about all that but it's still rather a nice *name*.

BEST FOOT FORWARD

All too seldom in life have I been able to pass on a valuable hint to those taking part in track events but now, with athletic meetings erupting all over everywhere, I can at last be of use. Here is my tip, and it is quite a simple one. On no account start waving to the crowd until you are safely past the post.

It is, you see, all a question of Wind Resistance. As a studious schoolboy at Oundle, I was well grounded in Physics (I think it was called Physics) and so Wind Resistance and I are old friends. The raising of the arms, the unclenching of the fists, the opening of the palms, the smile which widens the face — all these impede forward progress and are madness in an activity where the hundredth of a second can make just all the difference.

And what, may I ask, has happened to 'the tape'? In recent years the tape has completely vanished. How else can runners know that, and what a blessed moment it must be, they can stop running? The tape was always prominent in schoolgirl fiction: 'With a final desperate burst of speed, Mona's plimsolls thundered up the track and she breasted the tape a full foot in front of Monica. She had won, she had won! The coveted Bellingham Chalice was hers!'

The handling of sporting events by the television people is now totally masterly. How spoilt we are! There one is — right at Cram's shoulder, on horseback with Lester, at dear Mrs Lloyd's tennis elbow. And at golf they have now kindly taken to telling us, with a caption, what is happening ('Putting for a birdie'). Maybe this will spread to athletics — 'Trying to jump higher' and 'Struggling to run past the others'.

In the case of lady runners, a prominent bust is an obvious advantage. Burdensome though it may be while rounding that final bend, it comes into its own when, at the line, it catches the judges' eyes. I wonder whether, in her youth, Mae West ever took part in competitive sprints. In her case she would almost have won the race before it had even started.

Actually, this waving to the crowd to acknowledge athletic prowess is a relative novelty. Because of its appositeness, I draw attention once again to that famous episode in *The Black Gang* when adverse circumstances force Bulldog Drummond to throw his wife, Phyllis, over an electrified fence and she lands in a bush. Does she then waste time bowing to the public (it was midnight or thereabouts and so onlookers were few)? Not she! An example to all, she scampers off at once to find an un-vandalised telephone box and to warn Hugh's pals. As you'll recall, she had only recently been gassed outside the Ritz down a taxi's speaking tube, a useful facility now sadly denied us.

As to the high jump, in my day it would have been considered to be extremely eccentric, not to say showing-off, to jump over it backwards, let alone to land comfortably on a sort of trampoline thing. You jumped like a man, frontwards, and you landed, if you were lucky, in a sodden sand-pit, jarring every bone in your body. This was considered to be character-building, though what kind of character it built, who can say?

I've never really taken to an item called 'Putting the Weight'. It consists of nothing but bulging biceps, followed by a dismal thud. And at school it was not easy to know what to say by way of congratulation to the winner. A loud cry of 'Well put!' implies some sort of *bon mot* or verbal felicity far removed from muscles and thuds, and 'Well putted' takes one straight out onto the links. I usually settled for a manly 'Bravo!'

In order to try to shine at my prep school Sports Day, a merry boy called Williamson used assiduously to practise throwing the discus. He lived in a fantasy world and liked to imagine terrible disasters of various kinds for which he used to compose suitably dramatic headlines for the report in the *Hampshire Gazette*. I remember one which went HEADMASTER DECAPITATED IN FREAK DISCUS MISHAP. BOY APOLOGISES.

IT PAYS TO ADVERTISE

The managing director of Debrett's Peerage, bewailing the rising production costs in the book trade and fearful for the future of book publishers, has advised them to play for safety, copy Debrett's example, and take a leaf out of their book.

Or 400 leaves, to be precise, for it is this number of pages that the Peerage, which can be snapped up for a mere £45, devotes to every kind of advertisement — whisky, waders, woollies: you name it — and, what is more, *has been doing so since 1860*.

What a terrible waste of opportunities there has been elsewhere! As all telly addicts know, the advertisements are often the most rewarding part of the evening's viewing, and so it could have been with literature and, in particular, novels. Publishers with sense would dot their advertisements through the book so as to form a pleasing contrast to the other reading matter.

Thus, the widely admired but rather limp *Pluck Thou My Lyre Strings Gently* would have enormously benefited from having interleaved in it coloured encouragements to buy jumbo bottles of GUSTO ('The tonic that put the p's into pep'), with striking results, of the Before and After kind, of a Mr and Mrs O. Z. Tiplady of S.E.97 ('I owe my hubby's new-found vigour entirely to GUSTO').

Then, what about the somewhat esoteric *Sweet Lad o'Hellas*? This could have been gingered up with a few bathing beauties wearing the sensational BUSTO costume ('The swimsuit that clings but never cloys') while the rather daring *Their Love Brought Forth No Babe* (banned in Iran) would have been greatly cheered up by advertisements for beef stock and marrow-bone jelly and tinned shellfish in the rightly renowned LUSTO brand.

But stay, there is still time, for the classics are being constantly reprinted. I have recently been much impressed by an advertisement for a delightful occupation called Hot Tubbing, which seems to require a round redwood tub of generous dimensions, fitted with jets and full of both heated water and merrily smiling people.

Letting the underwater hydro-massage jets gently ease away the cares of the day

Hot tubbing might have made all the difference to the Macbeths. On arriving at the scene where Lady ('Daggers') Macbeth is harbouring thoughts that one can hardly applaud in a hostess, one turns the page and there is a Hot Tub and, in it and in the mind's eye, are Macbeth, his wife, Duncan and, if there's room, Banquo, all happily splashing away and 'letting the underwater hydro-massage jets gently ease away the cares of the day'.

I see so many pleasing and stimulating possibilities in the reprint world. Denture fixatives and bunion pads in *Wuthering Heights*. Aftershave lotion and Bermuda shorts in *Pride and Prejudice*. The wholesome tone of *Cranford* is by no means to everybody's taste and could be strengthened by a sprinkling of all the truly joyous things of modern life — computer dating, family planning and home massage kits.

I have to confess to a bit of a blank spot about the works of George Eliot, but something tells me that *Adam Bede* would be all the better for waterbeds, form-hugging jeans, nuclear shelters, cosmetic surgery, pine furnishings and micro-wave ovens.

Not all need be stimulation. Indeed, in certain cases a more relaxing mood is required. Take, for example, a best seller of the past, *The Sheik*, a thrilling work of fiction set amid the burning sands and fashioned for us by E. M. Hull, gifted wife of a Derbyshire pig-farmer who, it was said, had never been nearer to burning desert sands than the beach at Cleethorpes.

The heroine, proud Diana Kayo, finding herself alone in a tent with Sheik Ahmed Ben Hassan and wondering ('Lie still, you little fool') what plans he has for the next hour or so, could well do with the kind of advertisement that dampens ardour — 'WHY WEAR A TRUSS?', perhaps, or one of those that suggest a lack of personal freshness. 'Are you offending? Buy a luxi-sachet of WHIFFO, the body fragrance that lets you know it's there'.

I do hope the idea catches on. Chest-expanders in *Little Dorrit*. Colonic irrigation in *Hamlet*. The scope is immense.

HARDENING OFF

Flashing blithely to and fro as my busy work schedule dictates between London and Devon along the generously dualled A303, road of roads, and snug and warm within the car, the state of the outside temperature may be gauged by the number of sightseers gazing forlornly at what must be the world's second most uninteresting Object of Interest.

I refer of course to Stonehenge and I don't care a bit whether it does or does not date from the Bronze Age. On an icy February morning there was just the one crazed, camera-hung visitor and even from a distance one could sense his despair as he circled the deplorable stone lumps, clicking and snapping away at what must look even less engaging in colour photographs.

As months go, one simply cannot trust February to behave itself, a gloomy month which in the past has seen the start of the Indian Mutiny, the Massacre of Glencoe and the Reichstag going up in flames. Only the not-before-time beheading of Mary Queen of Scots has struck a really cheerful note. Volcanoes are well known to regard February as prime eruption time. We are not told the dates on which Nero put a match to Rome or when Lady Macbeth, a caring hostess if ever there was one, visited the Inverness spare room but you can bet your bottom groat it was February.

And this year, and with us down here in Devon, it has been 'February fill the dyke' my foot! Scarcely a drop of rain has fallen in the South, woodland areas are at fire risk and everywhere Water Authorities have been licking their greedy lips at the thought of the increased rates for their already highly-priced commodity, not to speak of the possibility of being able soon to announce a Drought and boss us all about with their emergency regulations.

I suppose that it was at English boarding-schools that, from the age of 9 to 18, one ran one's biggest risk of perishing from hypothermia. To be cold was to be manly. Water freezing in wash basins was very manly. Windows were for opening. And it was at prep schools that one waited to be told how best to face the chilly weather outside ('Please sir, is it overcoats?').

I had a fearless prep school contemporary called Williamson and it was his custom to test in various ways the patience of the school authorities. For example, when the headmaster was giving us an extra long harangue, Williamson liked to see how many smothered yawns he could get away with before the inevitable 'Oh do shut up, Williamson'. A further interesting test occurred when he slipped two fragrant bath cubes into his hot bath and stank the place out. But, beyond the master on duty saying 'Disgusting!', nobody could think of any reason why Williamson should be punished ('Oh do shut up, Williamson').

A lady, complete with a pianist confederate called Miss Midgeley, came once a week to teach dancing and to reveal to us the mysteries of the waltz, two-step and fox-trot. She called herself Madame Clermont but was about as French as Cockney rhyming slang. At the end of one lesson we were somewhat astonished when Williamson stepped forward and, with a courtly bow, presented her with a large bunch of chrysan-themums ('Oh you *dear* boy!'). They had been gathered by Williamson without permission from the extremely angry headmaster's garden and constituted yet another Test. The out-come? Six of the best and all pocket money confiscated.

Oh yes, about that least interesting Object. I had assumed in my simple way that, approaching by boat the harbour at Copenhagen, one would encounter that famous mermaid far out to sea, perched on a barren rock and bravely defying the roughest storms, drenched in spray and an example to all.

Not a bit of it. The feeble little creature sits safely on shore, indeed practically on the promenade itself and looking as though the most she plans is a brisk paddle at low tide with a shrimping net.

RIGHT AND LEFT

IN MOTION

If ever I were to write a novel, which God forbid as any offering of mine would be likely to be in the Instant Rejection class and would probably not even get further into the publishing hinterland of Messrs Tuckett and Clopthorne than pitiless Miss Rackstraw in Reception, I should doubtless find the same difficulties as some other novelists do in moving my characters about from place to place. My heroine would be a problem from the start. 'Felicity Freeborn caught the 8.15 for Market Lopton and changed at Darlington' is hardly a sentence with sparkle to it. On the other hand, if you just put 'On arrival at Market Lopton . . .', readers are going to ask themselves how anybody as feeble as Felicity managed to get herself there, Titian hair, dimples, freckles, cerise two-piece and all. Even moving characters quite short distances (Boots to the Co-op) would prove for me to be quite a puzzle.

Constant reading of the works of Sapper provides more than one example of an easy style that must be the envy of many. In his *The Dinner Club* (twelve splendid yarns told by various club members and published in the early 1920s) and in the story called 'Sentence of Death', the doctor relates that when the hero, Jack Digby, who wants to marry but has ticker trouble and is given two years at the most, comes into his Harley Street consulting room for the first time, 'I motioned him to a chair'. Look how simple that is! You just motion somebody and away they go! From a standing position, Jack Digby is all at once in a sitting position, even though he has shortly to jump up again (so bad for his heart) and remove, for examination purposes, his coat and shirt (which, while refreshing my memory, I have just managed to misread as 'skirt').

While admiring this smooth shuffling about of the dramatis personae, I have to confess that I don't tremendously care at any time for the word 'motion', either as a noun or a verb. 'Are you

215

beginning to feel the motion?' kind friends used to enquire
when the cross-Channel boat was a mere five hundred yards out
of Dover Harbour and one had already turned bright green and
was thinking of heading, with a loud 'excuse me', for the
bulwarks. 'Have you had a motion?' Matron used to ask, an
emergency mug of Gregory Powder at the ready, in the dorm,
totally mystifying the less literary boys who said yes they had
when it was sometimes no they hadn't. I am far from sure what
a Time and Motion study is and for all I know it may be an
enquiry into what should be a purely private affair, namely the
frequency of visit and duration of time spent there by employees
when making use of the lavatories. Let me hasten to exclude
from these matters the word Motion when used as a surname.
Indeed, and if memory serves, Queen Mary herself had at one
time a Lady in Waiting called the Lady Elizabeth Motion ('The
Lady Elizabeth Motion has left the Palace'), a name which here
inspires total confidence as a smoothly gliding presence, generally modestly in the background but always ready when needed
to dart forward and hold a handbag or pouch a posy or engage
in pleasurable chat ('*How* clever you've been with this house! I
can remember Groyne when it was virtually a ruin').

Well then, another of Sapper's yarns, 'The Pipes of Death',
begins dramatically with one of the club members, hand in the
tobacco-jar to prepare us for clouds of smoke and pauses while
'he puffed thoughtfully for a few moments', saying boldly
'Any of you know Burma?', a question which, post-war,
would find many sadly affirmative answers but which in 1920
was really quite something, few places being considered more
outlandish. It turns out that at least two of the fellow members
have been there (shooting tiger or planting tea or something
equally reputable) and before we know where we are we find
ourselves in 'the ruby mines in the Mandalay area', just as easily
as that — Pall Mall one minute and flying fish, temple bells,
native girls and the dawn coming up like thunder the next.
That's the way to do it. Had my Felicity Freeborn been bound
for Burma, I would first have sent her to the Berkeley Street
Cook's for her ticket and thence to the Sloane Street National
Westminster Bank for her foreign currency ('With a puzzled

little frown, Felicity tried to work out what £60 would come to in kyats'). How much more interesting to get her in a trice to the old Moulmein Pagoda of Kipling's and of which so many beefy baritones have sung (legs well apart and arms akimbo to indicate carefree manliness) with a view out to sea of 'the old Flotilla' proceeding along, apparently, with the aid of paddles, steam-driven ones, I assume, rather than those paddles in *Sanders of the River* that propelled Paul Robeson and that long and native-filled boat so speedily along (to shouts, when the film was shown in Oxford, of 'Well rowed, Balliol!').

But to return to motion as instanced in the concept of Perpetual Motion, those who recall, from their school days, a side-splitting joke to the effect that the phrase *pièce de résistance* was the French for constipation, should be able to do a similar bit of witty invention, of a converse nature, with Perpetual Motion (and, in poor taste as one's thoughts quite often are, I can never hear, from the musical comedy, *Véronique*, the hurrying, scampering, scurrying number which goes 'Trot here, trot there' without an instant visual image unintended by the lyricist). Nor have poets, even the best of them, been too careful about the words they use. The rightly revered Wordsworth wrote a poem, and in what some might think to have been a physically rather over-stimulated mood, called 'She Was A Phantom of Delight'. Just in case you don't happen to have the poem at command, let me refresh you as to the phantom's qualifications — 'a perfect woman, nobly planned' with dusky hair, eyes like stars at twilight, fairy-footstepped, full of strength, foresight and skill and just made 'for transient sorrows, simple wiles, praise, blame, love, kisses, tears, and smiles'. The poet also refers to 'her household motions light and free' — a handsome tribute to the generally smoothly functioning and healthy air that this 'lovely apparition' exudes and one to make the more sluggish of us envious in the extreme.

Only Freud would be capable of explaining why the word 'motion' goes so appallingly and obsessively to Wordsworth's head, or somewhere. He just cannot leave the thing alone. As there are nine references alone in the *Oxford Book of Quotations* (I'm speaking of the 1941 edition), heaven knows how many are to be found in the original poems (and I offer the idea as a dissertation possibility for some assiduous Eng. Lit. student). Some of the occasions on which the word is used are very ill-judged indeed. 'Everlasting motion', a very doubtful blessing, is referred to in 'The Prelude', and elsewhere we find 'eternal motion' (much the same thing, and nothing to encourage). Then there are 'sounds of undistinguishable motion', coupled with 'low breathings' and which, as all this is taking place 'among the solitary hills', gives an impression of hasty and unfortunate improvisations behind a gorse bush ('Ow!!'). As to the lady in 'A Slumber did My Spirit Seal', one's heart goes out to her in pity, for 'No motion has she now, no force'. Of the time when the poet allows the words motion and wind to appear in the very same sentence, I prefer not to speak.

When my novel appears, you won't find anybody motioning Felicity Freeborn either into or out of a chair, let alone anywhere else. Her motions in her Fulham bed-sitter will certainly be light and free as she flits from her gas-cooker ('tugging open the oven door, Felicity saw with relief that her toad-in-the-hole was starting to rise') to her transistor ('Hooray! Good old "100 Best Tunes" again!'), but I shall refer to them, not as motions, but as movements, though I'm not too sure that that word hasn't taken on, down the years, something of the meaning that motion has when it doesn't mean movement. If you follow me.

FOR THE RECORD

Every so often in our Devon village of Appleton the speed of social life slackens a little, the spate of visitors, always so welcome, at 'Myrtlebank' eases off a bit and I can devote myself for a space to intellectual matters and things of the mind (so muddling in childhood when officiating clergymen said in church 'Let us pray in silence for a space' and one wondered how large a space we were to pray for, and what the purpose of having such a space might be). And thus it was that on a recent Sunday evening I was able to devote myself to the full three hours of the telly showing of the film called *Star*, the Hollywood version of the life of Gertrude Lawrence, a film which failed, understandably, at the box office and did little to benefit the post-*Sound of Music* career of Julie Andrews (they kept making her fall comically over, which was neither her line nor Miss Lawrence's line nor at all funny). As regards her casting for the main role, Mr Coward, as he then was, had, as so often, the last word: 'If you don't have Julie for the part, whom *do* you have?' He was right. There was nobody else.

I do not propose to go in detail into the film, and it is not my province anyway, but it did contain for me such a moment of horror and inaccuracy that I felt, in fairness to the dear and dead performers, I must mention it. It was in 1924 that André Charlot took the three stunning stars whom he had nurtured and encouraged and managed, Beatrice Lillie, Jack Buchanan and Gertrude Lawrence, to America, three dazzling theatrical talents who burst triumphantly upon the New York public and were rightly a sensation. The film showed the American first night of this *Charlot's Revue* and, prior to the performance, one was appalled to see Mr Buchanan and Miss Lawrence on stage and peering through the centre of the curtain to watch the audience coming in ('Oh look, there's Alexander Woollcott!'). One winces in dismay. For one thing, 'Beginners please' would

219

not yet have been called and would anyway apply to the chorus and Mr B and Miss L would be still in their dressing-rooms, trying not be sick and planning suicide. And for another thing, any professional (and they truly don't come more professional than those two) would sooner die than do anything so unprofessional and amateur (and amateurs have largely given it up too). It is true that there is in most theatres a small slot or peep-hole right at the side through which the stage manager can see whether the house lights are out or if the conductor is in his place, or whatever. But that is all and, in their memory and having worshipped the ground that both these great stars walked on, I am glad to be able to put the matter right.

And, while in such a helpful mood myself, let me hasten to acknowledge gratefully a kind and helping hand over yet another matter of general interest. It may be recalled that in the past I made mention of the subject of car registration numbers and letterings and wondered whether or not words such as SOD and BUM and TIT were purposely avoided or were banned by some central Government adjudicator. I daresay that a number of you have been wondering about this but you need wonder no more. Everything in this field has now been made crystal clear to me by the greatly gifted Alec Bristow (many readers will remember his fascinating book, *The Sex Life of Plants*, a marvellous mixture of erudition and humour) who tells me that the onus of deciding what is tasteful and what is not tasteful is put upon local authorities. Each of them is issued with the last *two* letters of the car registration and then the providing of the initial letter is up to them. This amounts to a governmental let-out and a shifting of responsibility. Neat work, eh what?

In the county of Norfolk, to which had been allotted the letters EX, it seems that the local authority, clearly a thoroughly wholesome and right-thinking body, decided to skip straight from REX to TEX so that nobody, and oh the blessed relief of it, had to drive around labelled SEX. On the other hand, Essex, landed with OO, have gone boldly and fearlessly ahead with LOO, Mr Bristow having spotted several LOOs driving shamelessly about in the Braintree area. Who can doubt that the county has followed LOO up with such things as the pleasantly rural MOO and that contemptuous expression of disapprobation, BOO. It is to Leeds, which must surely be a district that positively pullulates with motor-cars, that the letters UM have been given and to which, therefore, the BUM decision has been, no doubt with complete confidence, left. And similarly to Grimsby has been entrusted the responsibility of deciding, faced with their letters which are EE, about, pardon me, PEE. I'm never quite sure what train-spotters jot down in those note-books — number of engine, whether buffy is open or not, colour of driver's eyes? Might they not find car-spotting equally interesting?

A few more sightings. Residents in Ayrshire, announcing themselves on their cars as HAG or BAG or LAG or NAG will know only too well that the letters AG were the ones provided, rather spitefully some might consider, for them. COW and SOW have gone to, of all the inoffensive towns to choose, Southampton, and I see with concern that it is onto dear old Devon that the letters OD have been off-loaded. Are they, having exhausted BOD and COD, now anxiously wondering how far off the day might be before the great SOD decision has to be made? If our local authority cares to get into touch with me (why not motor out for Elevenses?), I am quite willing, as an old head on old shoulders, to give them the benefit of my experience and advice.

DAY BY DAY

Although the *Encyclopaedia Britannica* is, as we know, the work of many gifted and scholarly hands and, to boot, a mine of valuable information should you require to bone up on whimbrels (a species of small curlew) or the humble glypton (fossils with fluted teeth), its varied contributors have cleverly managed to achieve between them a composite style, one of total and stultifying boredom. They should even be able , when the time arrives, to make a dullness out of the excitements of the Second Coming. Anything calling for expressions of feeling or heart or sensibility or warm understanding passes them by and nowhere more so than in the field of diaries, that most human of records. 'It is not necessary that the entries in a diary should be made each day', DAB-DUG pontificates, 'since every life, however full, must contain absolutely empty intervals.'

Rubbish! No interval is empty. Diarists, like everybody else, are for ever doing *something* — eating, sleeping, coughing, snoring, picking their teeth, hiccoughing — and it is this, the small change of life, that is so fascinating. The really important events in important lives automatically drift into the history books and are already known to us. We don't want to hear about Waterloo but what Napoleon ate after stumps were drawn ('The events of the day had somewhat put me off my food and I made but a poor supper').

The late nineteenth century, when time hung heavy on so many hands, is particularly fruitful in diaries. No reading is to me more riveting. One lives and breathes along with the writer. 'Heavy rain overnight, so wet underfoot. Put on my galoshes and went round to call on Canon Bilton. Bilton gone to Worcester for day, so returned home and took off galoshes.' There now! What a picture unfolds itself. The exciting expedition and the prudent precaution against damp, always such a hazard for the Victorians, followed by the sharp disappointment of finding no Bilton. We wonder, with the diarist, why the Canon has gone, or been summoned, to Worcester. A lightning dash to the ecclesiastical outfitters for a fresh set of canonicals? A surprise christening? An appearance before the magistrates as a result of a moment of madness behind the Violet Tea Rooms during that hot spell? We shall never know. And then the writer's return home, the sense of deflation, the sinking into a chair, the removal of the protective footwear. This is the very stuff of diaries. Those who, unlike the austere encyclopaedia, possess heart and feeling will rejoice to learn that a few days later the diarist comes upon Canon Bilton 'in the highest of high spirits' walking near Malvern which, though that town was perilously full of tea rooms, clearly reveals that there were in Worcester no grounds for prosecution.

Delightful evocations abound in the less well known diaries. The attractive Irish poet, Tom Moore, whose social gifts, melodious warblings among them, wafted him frequently into Holland House and elsewhere, found himself at a smart London gathering with Mrs Siddons. Leaning forward excitedly to hear what the renowned tragedienne might be discussing with Lady Castlereagh (the difficulty of playing Cleopatra? A new slant on Lady Macbeth?), he was able to catch the famous voice's first phrase: 'I do love ale dearly'. And across the years one's heart bleeds for an Oxford undergraduate called Hannington, mad keen on rowing, who one evening during the summer boat races found himself recording 'Of all atrocious horrors this is the most disgusting. We have been bumped by Keble'. Hannington became a missionary and, rashly venturing into East Africa, was briskly speared to death by the Masai tribe and presented as a *bonne bouche* to the hyenas, but this little mishap was clearly only one of life's pinpricks compared with that frightful day on the Isis.

And then there is little Scottish Anne Chalmers, aged seventeen, who kept a diary for just one year and was a fool for a dog-collar. 'I am very partial to English clergymen. They are very agreeable though generally of short stature.' She comes to London and raises her sights. 'I begin to like bishops very much. The Bishop of London is very handsome.' Taken to the

House of Lords, she feasts her eyes on 'the bench of bishops', subsequently meeting Bishop Wilberforce, known to all as

Little Scottish Anne Chalmers . . . was a fool for a dog-collar

'Soapy Sam' and a great one for hearing the first cuckoo, but finding him a bit of a let-down ('Unfortunately, his neck was so short'). What happened to Anne? Did she manage to ensnare a gaitered charmer with a long neck and marry him? Did they in turn beget bishops? Alas, the mists close.

Are all diary-keepers egotists? Not even the encyclopaedia dare face this question. It is certainly true that a lot of them are much concerned about their health and indeed I am able to pass on to hypochondriacs and health-faddists in general various remedies culled from diaries here and there which may prove efficacious in previously stubborn cases. To treat convulsions, apply dead pigeons to the head, and for nose-bleeding, hang a dried toad round the neck. For 'troubled bowels', brew a pot of Wainwright's tea and for griping spasms mix purgative drugs of aloes and aromatic bark. Then there is flatulence (don't stint the spinach), rheumatic pains (rub all joints with cider apples), cricked neck (hot plasters to the shoulder blades and shave the head) and sprained foot (apply snails). For 'weak and slow motions' I'm afraid there is nothing more practical suggested than prayer at night and morning.

MINOR ADJUSTMENTS

Is there somewhere in Whitehall, perhaps in an off-shoot of the Department of the Environment (of all meaningless and loony descriptions, surely the looniest), a group of devoted Government workers, knee-deep in cups of tea and M.B.E.s and surrounded by *Chambers*, whose task it is to dream up the least suitable name possible for whatever new feature of life may come along? They started strongly way back with the invention of DUAL CARRIAGEWAY, presumably meaning roads down which only hackney-carriages, or vehicles let out for hire, may travel two abreast. Whoever now connects 'carriage' with anything but a train or a typewriter or a tightly-corseted lady ('She has a very fine carriage')? The two words (the Americans opted sensibly for DIVIDED HIGHWAY) have the ring of a sedate and upper-crust Edwardian couple living in comfortable circumstances in Kent ('. . . the occasion being graced by the presence of Sir Dual and Lady Carriageway').

Then what of SOFT VERGES? 'Verge' is hopelessly antiquated except in the sense of 'I am on the verge of going right off my nut'. Why not CRUMBLY SHOULDERS? And with verges, allied to soft, there is the added danger of over-exciting any hot-blooded male Frenchman abroad and on our roads, the word verges being all too close to the seductive *vierges* of which every frog worth his salt dreams. Whoever is responsible for all this idiocy came a good old cropper a few years ago with, at roundabouts, the word YIELD which, although somehow redolent of romantic fiction ('Yield to me, Blanche'), meant really nothing to anybody and which had to give way to, indeed, GIVE WAY, an activity that ladies recently widowed are always being urged not to indulge in ('My dear, you *mustn't* give way').

There is, however, one sign that combines total clarity with the utmost in the way of unhelpfulness. It is the one that warns of danger ahead and announces that the road down which you are happily bowling is liable, at a moment known only to God, to subside beneath your wheels and, presumably, plunge you down into a crevasse or a disused mineshaft or some abandoned sewers or drains. What, I always wonder, are we supposed to do on sighting this alarming piece of information? Stop, backtrack and take that B road through Chumley Bottom? Proceed forwards with the greatest caution, eyes peeled for cracking, heaving tarmac? Or drive as fast as the car allows, to reduce the time spent on the road and thereby lessen the risk, remembering that mathematicians inform us that, at infinite speed, the car would never actually be on the road at all? The notice is, I suspect, a legal safeguard by the crafty local council, enabling them to say a haughty 'But we told you so' when your mini is wrong side up and twenty feet down and you are still trying to extract Cousin Madge, in considerable disarray, from the back seat. During the subsequent attempt to obtain damages, one can picture all too clearly the unspeakably irritating legal shenanigans in court: 'How came you to be on this road when you had received a clear warning of its danger?'

My first experience of what seemed at the time like twaddle official instructions came in North Devon when I was quite young. After bathing in the icy-cold rock pools for which Ilfracombe is famous, I could locate no lavatory by the sea-shore and so, on my way back to my grandparents' house, I nipped in to a Gentlemen's conveniently situated at the crossroads. As I was about to re-emerge, I found myself confronted by a large notice which said KINDLY ADJUST YOUR DRESS BEFORE LEAVING. Dress? What dress? Only women wore dresses. Was it possible that, blinded by physical demands, I had darted by mistake into the Ladies'? A moment's anxiety and then I remembered the splashy stalls that I had just left and, remembering too the fact that ladies sat down, breathed again. The introductory word 'Kindly' was very off-putting. Whenever it was directed at one, it spelt trouble: 'Kindly behave yourself'. 'Kindly remember where you are'. And the word 'adjust' was a problem. How could anybody adjust a dress. You just put the thing on and it hung there, for better or worse. Totally perplexed, I scuttled hurriedly out and made for home.

Never learning from experience, it was my practice to air puzzlements and ask for guidance when we were all gathered together at tea-time. My grandfather, being a clergyman, seemed to me to be ideally placed for providing Guidance, spiritual or purely practical as the need might be. And so, taking courage and deciding to over-look the fact that anything in any way connected with lavatories was considered to be indelicate, I popped my question, struggling for a hearing against the general scrunching sounds made by cucumber sandwiches being loudly bitten into and softened up for their final slithering down the red lane. There was, as usual, some little difficulty in making myself understood, and when understood I was not, again as usual, a popular figure. Amid all the frownings and tut-tuttings, nobody, of course, volunteered an explanation but later a kind uncle showed himself to be in agreement and promised to write to the town council and suggest that the notice should be changed to read BEFORE LEAVING PLEASE ENGAGE ALL TROUSER BUTTONS SECURELY AND RETURN HANDS TO NORMAL POSITION. He may, I see now, have been joking.

PARDON MY TWITCH

We live and learn and it's never too late, I suppose, to add to one's towering storehouse of knowledge but I never thought that, so late in life, the information would reach me that Sir Richard Burton had a morbid fear of honey. Moreover, even if a fragrant canister of the best Bee-Zee-Bee were concealed in a cupboard behind a strong-smelling pickle jar, he could still sense its presence there and demand its instant removal. Our informant is his wife, and life, one feels, was already sufficiently complex for poor Lady Burton without finding herself landed with a honey phobic spouse. Doubtless the cause goes back to some unfortunate episode in childhood. Was he, do you think, stung painfully by a swarm of bees and a victim thereafter of Apiphobia? Was he possibly punished too severely for raiding the store-cupboard and pinching the delicious substance, the subsequent harsh flogging bringing with it Mastigophobia (a dislike, natural enough, of being flogged)? Lady Burton, who had good reason not to enquire too closely into any of her husband's activities, is silent on this point. She was, perhaps, more fortunate than she knew. There are trickier things than honey. Robert Benchley once confessed to suffering from Genuphobia or, as he preferred to call it, 'Kneephobia', a fear that his knees were suddenly going to start bending the wrong way. But Benchley was a distinguished humorist and may well not have been entirely serious.

Sympathetic persons, seeking a kind explanation for Queen Victoria's outstandingly unacceptable behaviour after the death of Albert, hiding herself grumpily away and refusing to earn her keep, have decided that the shock of his departure brought with it the well-known Agoraphobia, originally 'fear of the market place' and a region that she would be hardly likely to grace but which has come to mean a general irrational fear of open places and of the many disasters that may occur in them, the vast majority of these particular phobics being women. Kind Joy Melville, in her *Phobias and Obsessions*, is all explanation and helpful advice about treatment of this and many another distressful complaint. But, all the same, it's quite clear to me that, in the case of Victoria, she merely went into a tremendous thirty-year sulk against the Almighty over the removal of Albert, a reliable husband, if ever there was one, in the boudoir. Agoraphobia my foot!

The phobic possibilities are tremendously varied and perhaps one might make oneself just that little bit more interesting by developing one or two that are fully suitable to one's personality. What about, for instance, Linonophobia, or fear of string? Difficult to bring into really effective play because nowadays there isn't all that amount of string about, parcels arriving so heavily cellotaped (and *that* would make a much better phobia) that, as with packets of biscuits, you have to fight your way furiously in. Or there is Metallophobia (fear of metals) which could set one twitching excitingly in other people's motor-cars ('I say, are you feeling all right?'). Elaborate opening of windows and fannings of face, and then, 'Do please forgive this silly old phobia of mine. It'll pass. Let's just pull into that pub over there for a while'. Which leads us on to Demonophobia or fear of spirits, which is not a thing I suffer from, whatever spirits this phobia may have in mind.

A number of the phobias mentioned I discover that I already possess, among them Autophobia, or fear of oneself. At a not very advanced hour, I dart to the bathroom glass, and say, can you see by the dawn's early light what further imperfections, another crease here, a bulge there, nature has gleefully dabbed on during the night. But, depressing sight though I may present, it's the mechanism inside my head that I fear the most and which increasingly produces absent-mindedness (wellies carefully put away in the fridge), literary laziness (I have a really advanced dread of novels, or 'Irisophobia'), and forgetfulness of names ('Yes, yes, but whose Jubilee?'). I find that I don't at the moment happen to suffer from Auroraphobia, or fear of auroral lights, Triskaidekaphobia (a fear of being thirteen at table or, indeed, of having to stammer that word out), Anemophobia (wind — that of heaven, presumably), Stasiphobia (fear of standing upright, and a real beast), or Aulophobia (fear of the sound of flutes), but they can count me in when it comes to Gallophobia (distrust of all things French), and Spheksophobia (wasps) and I'm right there with Lord Beeching when our old friend Siderodromophobia rears its head (it means a dislike of railways, even to the point of removing them completely). I used to have, in childhood and especially at mealtimes and when invited to eat it, a slight attack of a phobia mysteriously not mentioned here. It was 'Lettucephobia' or fear of lettuce. Perhaps Miss Melville may care to include it in a further volume. The cure and treatment were simplicity itself. Remove the lettuce.

Fear of spiders (Arachnophobia) is, despite their relatively small size and retiring ways, modestly carrying on in quiet corners and minding their own business, widespread, even though superstitious rhymes about them are largely in the spider's favour: 'Kill a spider, bad luck yours will be, Till of flies you've swatted fifty-three'. The idea (spread about by Shakespeare, I regret to say) that they are venomous is incorrect and they have positively been credited with certain medicinal virtues (and here all serious Arachnophobics had better leave us for a few lines). A common cure for jaundice was to swallow a large, live house spider wrapped in butter. The same remedy put paid to ague in Ireland. In cases of fever (admittedly in 1760), munch a spider either wrapped in a raisin or spread upon bread and butter. For whooping cough, just hold a spider by the leg over the patient's head with a glad cry of 'Spider as you waste away, Whooping cough no longer stay'. For rheumatism, pop a handful of cobwebs between two slices of apple, sugar to taste and bring to table.

But it's nice to feel that, as regards one phobia listed here, we are all at least in the same boat, an extremely nasty boat though it may currrently be. We all have this phobia as we struggle to live, to keep going somehow, to put up with shoddy behaviour from our alleged betters, to endure insults (everybody's so cross, and getting crosser), to be sneered at by every other country, ill-led by non-leaders, over-taxed and over-tired. I'm not by nature a pessimist but I do find myself sighing a good bit as day follows day. You'll want to know the name of the phobia. It's Panophobia. It just means 'fear of everything'.

In cases of fever . . .

MOTHER O' MINE

I wonder whether anybody has recently been sparing any sort of sympathetic and friendly thought for Goethe's mother. She seems to be so terribly out of things these days though it is true that she did leave us rather a long time ago, in 1808. I ask, because in this year's elaborate jollifications over the anniversary of Beethoven's death (and I fail, incidentally, to grasp the special magic of the figure of 150), Frau Beethoven, the only reputable Frau in his life, for he never married, has come in for what some might consider more than her rightful allowance of attention. After decades of neglect, she suddenly became the Mother of the Year. Flowers were strewn on her grave, grateful prayers were offered up for her in churches and her name was on almost everyone's lips.

Goethe's 150th comes up in five years' time, in 1982. Can't we make it a real rouser too for dear old Mrs Goethe? After all, she did achieve a certain kind of immortality, for two reasons. Firstly, she produced one of the world's most renowned writers and *penseurs* and she herself can hardly be blamed for the fact that her son's clever pen carried with it more than its fair share of annihilating ennui (if you don't believe me, rattle through *Faust Part II* in the original and see how you get on). And secondly, she got herself unwittingly into numerous anthologies of famous Last Words. Invited to tea by friends unaware of how seriously ill she was, she sent a polite message back declining and adding that she was 'busy dying'. I do not know what Frau Beethoven gasped out as the grim reaper loomed up, nor do I wish to. Let her now return, so to speak, whence she came.

Herr Goethe senior is, alas, a somewhat shadowy figure but perhaps it is just as well. What one might call literary fathers make on the whole a pretty poor showing. We all know of the unsatisfactory nature of Dickens' dad. Closer to the present day

233

there has been the colourful figure of Sir George Sitwell, seemingly quite unaware of the brilliance of the children he had hatched and who merely kept wailing what a pity it was that his daughter Edith had never 'taken up' lawn tennis. Even in his eighties, Balzac's lustful old father was still active and vigorous among what must have been a singularly geriatric-geared bevy of village maidens. The examples of unfortunate and inadequate paternity are endless. Were some of them unconsciously driven to eccentric and defiantly show-off behaviour in a desperate effort to reassert themselves? It is, as history reveals, very difficult for some fathers to stomach the fact that their sons are going to be of far greater interest and importance than they ever were themselves. Mothers take such discomfitures calmly and, indeed, welcome them. Pride in their children, so often denied to egocentric fathers, keeps them going. And there is often more light and shade in mothers than in the male breadwinners.

Of whom would one's First XI of agreeable and unusual literary mums consist? High in the batting order comes Edward Marsh's mother, Jane, who was tone-deaf. Asked to identify a piece of music that was being played, she replied briskly that as far as she was concerned it was either 'God Save the Weasel' or 'Pop Goes the Queen'. Boxed on the ear for some childish offence, she at once boxed herself on the other out of a love of symmetry. Then there was James Lees-Milne's mother and her passion for ballooning. If a balloon chanced to put down near her, she could be counted on to climb speedily into the basket and be borne loftily away, sometimes for a full week's absence. Richard Church's parents (and if you haven't read *Over The Bridge* get it at once) met under an umbrella on a soaking day in Cheyne Walk, his grandfather being one of those domestic tyrants who, not liking the look of a mutton-chop, would hurl it moodily into the fire. There was no moodiness about entrancing Mrs Church, rattling out her *valses brillantes* in spirited sessions at the bogus-sounding Broadwood-White pianoforte and, with the greenest fingers in the whole of S.W.11, defiantly surrounded by flowering flower-pots and assorted greenery in the middle of Victorian Battersea.

At a different position on the social ladder we find Lord

Berners' mother, a charming creature who was only really happy and fully at home on a horse, possibly because it provided a convenient means of escape from her father, who sat all day long in a darkened room emitting a never-ending stream of loud groans and curses (his occasional visits to church caused alarm among the officiating clergy as their sermons were apt to draw forth a crescendo of violent oaths, upon which there was a scamper to the altar, the Blessing was hastily pronounced, and the congregation rapidly dispersed, looking anxiously over its shoulder).

What sort of assessment can one make, I wonder, of Shakespeare's mother? The known facts are meagre indeed and it is extremely unfortunate that in the Bard's day the word 'mother' also meant either 'an apparatus for chicken-rearing' or 'the disease of hysteria' and all the emotional instability that goes with it. Quite so. It is therefore hardly surprising that some of the mothers in the plays don't rate many marks out of 10. If we knew where to look, I expect that the Danish records would show that Queen Gertrude, a deeply unsuitable mother and indolent and sex-obsessed into the bargain, made but a poor showing as President of the Elsinore Women's Institute, muddling lecturers' dates and losing the key of the petty-cash box. Lady Macbeth has 'given suck', as she is the first to inform us and in a somewhat immodest manner, and so must have had at least one child, but whatever became of it, may one enquire? She was, she tells us further, quite ready in certain circumstances to 'dash the brains out', and what kind of motherly conduct is that? I have never personally been too happy about the culinary ingredients that went into the steaming hotpot that graced, as the principal *plat*, the Banquet in Act III that was such a social flop. Plenty of herbs and veg, of course, but what else to give it, unfortunate word, *body*? As a hostess, Lady Macbeth would, as we know, stick at nothing.

And whatever can one make of Queen Lear, deserting the sinking ship and abandoning a husband who is plainly going rapidly dotty, together with three daughters, two of whom are obviously becoming 'handfuls'? Her refusal to show up at all must have been very wounding. She probably hooked it, and who could really blame her, to some quite healthful resort (Bognor) with a doughty Knight and the scandal was hushed up, with possibly a false announcement of her death. Not a reputable mother, anyway. As you see, white-haired old Mrs Goethe has much to recommend her and is an example to all.

STILL YET MORE
SUNDAY BEST

FOR THY STOMACH'S SAKE

The news, excitingly flashed to us by the Wine Development Board, whoever and wherever they may be (I seem to see them at Ferment House, Vine Street, EC3) that women's purchases of wine now exceed those of men, will greatly cheer those of us who from time to time happily dine out with married couples.

Two heads being, as is widely claimed, better than one, you can be confident that now either the husband or the wife or both will have remembered to chill the Barsac and let the Nuits-Saint-Georges breathe, or whatever, and to order an ample sufficiency of each.

There is of course nothing new in women taking a lively interest in wine. While some home-made wines make one thoughtful (the proudly uttered remark 'We trod the grapes ourselves' prepares one for a rather distinctive bouquet), Women's Institute members have for years been constructing delicious bottles of this and that, parsnip and elderberry being especially recommendable.

The Old Testament bristles with references to persons of both sexes putting the stuff away or causing others to do so, achieving various results not all of which make suitable Sunday reading. And those who wonder why Noah's first act, the moment the ark touched down, was to take a restorative glass of wine, or two, or three (probably a roughish claret) and then pass quietly out, may have forgotten the presence at his elbow of Mrs Noah, gently urging on her Man of the Year ('Sip away, dear, you owe it to yourself').

I suppose that the first woman to make really practical use, career-wise, of wine was Lady Macbeth. One wonders what heady brand so totally befuddled Duncan's hapless attendants. St Emilion would not have 'travelled' at all well to Inverness and would certainly have lost much of its potency and so, in the servants' hall, she is likely to have served a reputable Beaune or even a rich Château Margaux with bags of body.

Incidentally, although scholars have hitherto been puzzled about the exact nature (Brandy-and-soda? Marsala? Port?) of Macbeth's nightcap — 'Go bid my mistress, when my drink is ready, She strike upon the bell' — it is now generally accepted in academic circles that the drink in question was Bournvita. With so many muddled heads about, Macbeth would not even have risked a small jigger of Sandeman or Best Cockburn at that tricky stage of the evening's proceedings.

What, one so wonders, did they all drink at dinner? Doubtless vermouth aperitifs were served beforehand on the ramparts (such a *view!*), and perhaps Lady Macbeth then gave them a Chablis with smoked salmon. The main *plat* can hardly have been anything but a jumbo haggis and so I dare say (and one can see the hostess's resigned look) they all swigged Scotch.

Another problem arises with, during that lively fencing match at the end of *Hamlet*, the stoups of wine available for the combatants. Poisoned or not, it would have had to be a variety to tempt not only the somewhat sweaty fencers, with the poor old Prince puffing quite a bit, but also Queen Gertrude herself, a lady with, obviously, an educated palate. I tend to think that the wine was a refreshing Hock or Hock-type, but I am open to correction.

The fact that in the works of Miss Angela Brazil there is very little reference to drink of any kind, even lemonade, does not mean that wine was not available. The superbly practical Miss Brazil would have been fully in favour of its moderate use as a corrective or a tonic. When, during *Loyal to the School*, the headmistress, Miss Tatham, of Northfield (head girl, Lesbia Ferrars: school colours, maroon and puce) conks completely out with exhaustion at the end of an unusually taxing Winter Term, one somehow senses that her first act on recovering will to be order for herself a crate of Wincarnis. And very nice too.

The end of an unusually taxing Winter Term

RICHTER RUMBLES

How very characteristic of our conscientious Prime Minister to be able, during what must have been an exceptionally taxing schedule abroad, to find time to give us a lead in an important social matter. As an arbiter in things requiring taste and refinement she has no equal and the guidance to which I refer was flashed to us in a newspaper headline, the information itself coming from the very heart of Mexico City where she has recently been representing us.

The headline, I hasten to say, was not one of those intended to shock and disturb. Older readers may recall that some years ago there was a literary competition which invited competitors to produce invented headlines which would really make everybody gasp. The winning entry ran ARCHDUKE FRANZ FERDINAND STILL ALIVE, GREAT WAR FOUGHT BY MISTAKE. Further sick jokes followed: QUEEN TO TAKE UP VIVISECTION and TITANIC FLOATS TO THE SURFACE WITH NOBODY THE WORSE FOR THEIR DUCKING.

The headline referring to Our Leader was essentially of a calming nature, particularly for hostesses with a busy programme of lunch and dinner parties ahead and with exciting ideas about food. It just said MRS THATCHER IGNORES RUMBLINGS.

There now! A definitive judgement at last about what to do at that awkward moment when noises that are not conversation break out round the table, noises that a tactful host tries sometimes ('They *said* it would be thundery!') to cover up with chat ('There goes another jumbo lorry!'). No need for that now. Just ignore.

There are, of course, those know-alls who will protest that the rumblings mentioned in connection with Mrs Thatcher's Mexican trip were those occasioned by an earthquake which, arriving unbidden at our Ambassador's dinner party (furniture waltzed about but they all munched courageously on), registered 6.4 on the Richter Scale. But earthquakes, though an undoubted nuisance, are purely regional matters and I choose to interpret the headline in this altogether wider sense of a noisy gastric readjustment and how best to deal with it.

I have no really deep knowledge of what types of food grace a Mexican table but something tells me that they are one and all spicy and alarmingly rumbleprone. Beans in any shape or form are dicey stuff and what is Chilli con carne but a 16oz can of red kidney beans in which a few explosive etceteras such as onions and garlic figure prominently. Nobody can tell me that Mexican Pumpkin Soup doesn't possess dangers all its own. They eat rice with onions and *frijoles* (fancy name for beans). The recipe for Mexican Meatballs is disquieting in the extreme. But grateful we must be to Mexico for providing the appropriate kind of gastronomic background for Mrs Thatcher's firm stand.

For many years now I have had my own personal Richter Rumbling Scale. Although I know that the Beaufort Wind (not to be confused with Rumbling) Scale goes up to 12, I have never discovered what Richter goes up to. My own Scale goes up to 20 and, just to give you an example, stewed gooseberries are rated 18 while, at the other end, rice pudding is 2. Rollmops? 14. A charming family of my acquaintance refers to the internal physical convulsions that often accompany the rumblings as 'troop movements' and indeed on occasions it feels as though Waterloo itself is about to begin.

I think it odd that no previous Prime Minister has seen fit to speak out so loudly and clearly on the social conundrum of what to do for the best when such audibilities occur. Mr Heath, for example, did his full share of entertaining when at No. 10 and would appear to be a fine trencherman but, nice and polite man that he is, I rather place him in the 'Oooops!' and 'Pardon' world. The newspapers, for some reason, spared us no detail of Sir Harold's *cuisine*, a *cuisine* that can hardly have been rumbleproof, but never a word was said. Churchill and Gladstone both have the look of having been pretty potent rumblers, but were silent, in this sense, about it.

Not a whisper out of any of them and a further proof, if one were either needed or wanted, of the unique nature of the hostess of No. 10.

CAPITAL!

Those of us who aren't currently compelled, by reasons of work or shopping (suddenly finding ourselves right out of pilchards in tomato sauce and tasty 'cod in the bag') or the claims of Dan Cupid, to make our way to London, would do well to remain just where we are. Our poor grubby capital is now increasingly reserved for foreigners — the only ones who can afford its prices — and it is jammed with mysterious orientals from end to end. In the silent film days, all orientals were up to no good at all, and some of us oldies just can't shake off the idea.

> In our own little garden subbub
> Away from the noise and the hubbub

People used to sing (it was a song popular at about the same time as 'Yes, we have no bananas', surely the world's least rewarding ditty) and though hubbub seems now to have caught up with some subbubs, my advice to those who live in them is 'Stay there'.

In London one now becomes, for one thing, merely a series of signposts. In a Kings Road bus queue, a German lady edged up to me and said ingratiatingly 'I am coming with you to St Paul's?' In Victoria, a dazed Indian politely asked for directions to the Isle of Dogs. On Millbank, a dusky carload enquired whether they were right for Wembley. It was midday. 'Drive north', I cried, 'and try to keep the sun behind you. Good luck!' and off they bravely shot towards Putney.

Recently, Her Majesty, feeling hospitably inclined, invited a few friends to have tea with her in her garden, as anybody might do. To allow them to reach the Palace in a reasonably fresh condition and before the last of the paste sandwiches and fairy cakes had been gobbled down, the police diverted else-where those not invited but also awheel. At the same time, officialdom in its wisdom closed half of the Hyde Park Corner underpass, and the traffic lights at the top of Sloane Street failed. There was a monumental, and what a fitting word it is, snarl-up.

As a result of it, I found myself trapped for half an hour on the top floor of a No. 19 bus and with a large collection of assorted foreigners, maps spread. Near me a mixed party of Dutch were muttering what, in that weirdest of languages, sounded like a string of deplorable obscenities but which were doubtless just requests for matches or cries of appreciation at the tasteful façade of Harvey Nichols or prudent reminders such as 'Don't let me forget my umbrella', which sounds, I suspect, perfectly filthy. A French lady by my side was much put out by the delay. 'Vy is zis bus not being on the move?' she asked, rather too haughtily for my liking. 'Your guess is as good as mine' I rather snappily replied then relented and added in a courteous translation *'Votre conjecture est aussi bonne que la mienne'*. She looked bemused. I felt that as an explanation, *'Madame la Reine donne un de ses "garden-parties"'* would have been disloyal.

It was of course the war that first brought foreigners in bulk to London (and thank heaven for them and their courage) and they have been here, more or less welcomely, ever since. I would feel more charitably disposed to them all if some of the middle eastern ones were less seldom found in what is discreetly called 'a noted Oxford Street store' trying to stuff fourteen unpaid-for cardigans up their burnouses prior to exiting unobserved. Arrested, they are found to be carrying untold wealth about their persons. There is an argument here for an on-the-spot re-introduction of the stocks (you can count on me to shy the first rotten egg) or alternatively whatever punishment they would find most unacceptable (bastinado, hand-chopping, impalement, removal of various accessories) in their own rather less feeble countries.

With some of us who, like me, live happily in the past and hurry thither frequently, the mind flashes back to the days when a foreigner in London, outside of the East End and its imagined opium dens and wily Chinese luring moon-faced

English roses to a life of leisure, or something, on their sampans, was a relative rarity. Tidily dressed people trod the clean pavements. Shoes shone. You could sit down and rest in an ABC over buns and tea (nowadays, to rest weary bones, it has to be a rather whiffy Jiffyburger). Nobody sold sex in shops or advertised 'assisted showers' and no jumbo coaches fouled up Piccadilly Circus and its environs. Policemen on foot were seen (and seen to be seen) and old ladies emerging from a performance of *George and Margaret* ('My dear, we all absolutely *roared*') could walk down side-streets without getting hit on the head and robbed by contemptible youths working, and how stout-hearted of them, in gangs.

. . . they are found carrying untold wealth about their persons

But away with such gloomy and unprofitable thoughts for in the mind's eye there is still Jack Buchanan at the Hippodrome, an upper circle matinée seat waiting to be filled, and curried prawns to be munched to an orchestra at the Corner House.

LABEL WITH CARE

There is much to be said for allowing children, when they have reached riper years and can tell a Mars bar from a Smartie, to change the perfectly frightful Christian names that they have often been landed with at the font, a spot where parents are frequently shown at their inconsiderate worst and usually sheltering in a craven manner behind Godmothers and Godfathers.

Who can doubt that when a baby screams ever louder and appears to be about to go into convulsions, it is not the cold water or the indignity of being poked at by a stranger that have annoyed it but the fact that it has just heard that it has henceforth to face Life while being called Euphemia Berenice or Algernon Makewater, names made all the more unacceptable by the fluting and parsonical tones in which they have been uttered.

You can change surnames (and we shall be coming to them in a moment) at will it seems, though on payment of a fee, but not the others. God-given, I suppose, and so no swopping. But how joyous at, say, the age of eight to change Percy for Jason, Maud for Tracy and Edith for Cindy Lou.

Then there is the important matter of initials. I myself was saddled with initials that formed a three-letter word, not a very offensive one to be sure but the fact was not noticed until, the deed done, they were all back in the house and celebrating ('Who's for another hock-and-seltzer?'). In church I am said to have screamed violently and to have struck gamely out at the Rev. Sheepshanks, but then who with spirit wouldn't?

Other initial-holders have been less lucky. At school one of the agreeable chaplains was called Wilfred Cole, and many school-masterly notices on notice boards merely require initialling. At prep schools, it was the accepted thing, and perhaps still is, to have your initials in large black letters on your tuck-box and, while teasing them mercilessly, one's heart went out to

249

Paul Igram Grantly and Francis Andrew Trevelyan and Arnold David Arbuthnot. And they were the more fortunate ones.

At school one lived in dread that a hitherto concealed name (one of mine was Bertram) would see the light of day. Entry forms for examinations required full names and were often filled in in class by the master and with particulars supplied verbally by the boy and out would pour, to their owners' consternation, the Clarences and the Theodores and the Marmadukes. And here let us cast a sympathetic glance at Peregrine, which cannot have made life easy.

As to surnames, recent correspondence has revealed some bizarre ones, capable of a variety of misspellings, and a few years ago there was that splendid American compilation with its names which, although guaranteed genuine, seemed to have come from some wild and make-believe world — Bambina Broccoli, Ophelia Legg, Osborn Outhouse, and Silence Bellows (one time Editor of the *Christian Science Monitor*). There were shorter ones too: O. Hell and Tee Hee.

For a more sober (and far more reliable) supply of quaint surnames, one naturally turns to the London Telephone Directory. Who in their right mind would dream of accusing those revered pages of harbouring lies and falsities?

You are probably as fond as I am of that vintage year and of the four 1936 volumes of the directory, the pages of which one lovingly turns when wanting a good read. Although in those days there were fewer telephones (and a good thing too), there are still treasures galore to be found. For starters, how about a call to Mrs Enid Trampleasure of Putney, or on getting, for so popular is she, the engaged burr-burr signal, switching to Mr Golightly of Streatham? Elsewhere there are to be found a Mrs Squance, a Miss Splitter and nice old Mr Smellie. The letter P, such a mine of good things, provides families called Ponking.

This was in the telephonic days when 405 was HOL and 589 was KEN and 730 was dear old SLO. There were letters as well as numbers on the dial and sometimes they formed a useful word to remember a number by. A friend of mine could be rung by dialling KEN DONT, and a famous actress was startled to find that her friends were remembering her as FLAGBAG.

BAGS I!

One of the many problems connected with clothes is that friends, acquaintances, public figures and people pursuing this or that profession get so very much fixed in one's mind as being dressed in a certain way that we consider clothing changes in others to be unacceptable. Any variation, even the smallest, is pounced on and greeted mentally with a critical 'What *has* she got on!'

The winged collar revealing the wobbly Adam's apple, the drab businessman's suit topped by the Homburg hat, were the making (for what it was worth) of Chamberlain. What if he had returned from Berchtesgaden and the Hitler visit in jaunty Tyrolean rig and, in his elation at that paper promise, had gone into one of those shoe-slapping dances. We wouldn't have known which way to look. Furthermore, we wouldn't have believed a word he had to say (even with the winged collar still intact, some of us at the time didn't believe a lot of it as it was).

Well then, removing her for once from that armour and the chariot with the bescythed wheels, how does the idea grab you of Boadicea floating about in a filmy apricot tea-gown and doing the honours at a Camulodunum barbecue ('*Do* let me spear you another sausage!')?

What of the conception of Queen Mary in a trim pair of running shorts? How about Florence Nightingale in goggles and all kitted out for the Cresta run? Or Joan of Arc in see-through pyjams? They would, after all, be the same people underneath, and yet, somehow, not.

We are fortunate in the fact that when the subject of schools and suitable clothing for schoolmistresses rears its head, we have a supreme arbiter of scholastic good taste to whom we can fly. I am of course referring to Miss Angela Brazil and the members of the teaching profession who figure so prominently in her matchless schoolgirl stories.

251

Not that Miss Brazil, with so much excitement afoot elsewhere, can afford to linger very long on her staffs' clothes, but here and there is a hint or two and illustrations to help us. For example, Miss Whitlock in *At School With Rachel*, through whose snuggery window a forbidden tennis ball has just come whizzing, is to be seen looking tremendously ratty in pince-nez, a voluminous skirt in deepest brown, a sateen blouse with collar and tie in the school colours (apple green and magenta), and a no-nonsense hair-do.

Boadicea . . . doing the honours at a Camulodunum barbecue

'Winter petticoats' get a mention in *The Third Class at Miss Kay's*, and though the wardrobe of dear Miss Suffolk, co-principal in *Jean Goes to School*, is not, alas, revealed to us, one can *sense* the faultlessly cut tailor-made in a darkish fawn. Miss Thompson, headmistress of a school quaintly called Silverside, is shown to us ticking off a blubbing junior in a tube-like sort of skirt, an open-necked blouse (silk by the look of it) and a serviceable lanyard, while Miss Cartwright of St Cyprian's, seen pinning up on the notice-board the name of the Monitress elected to be responsible for inkwells, also favours a severe full-length skirt relieved by a rather showy cardigan.

Not that Miss Brazil, a great realist who moved with the times, would have had, so to speak, anything against trousers. She did not die until after the war and, while travelling about, would have been as delighted as the rest of us by those sturdy women railway porters (and where oh where have they gone?) who naturally strode about in trousers. Highly practical, Miss Brazil would, I am convinced, have been in favour of trousering certain members of her staff. One of her botany mistresses conducting a nature ramble and scrambling about in hedgerows and ditches in search of bladderwort and the more hideous sorts of fungi (is it my imagination or was there one of them called 'Queen Edith's Lapse'?), would have found bags a great boon. She could have whipped them off before joining the others at cocoa.

Of one thing we can be quite sure. Miss Brazil was no fool and she would never have permitted any illustration which showed a bebagged member of her staff from the rear. Only the slimmest of the slim can survive this test (perhaps it would be wise for headmasters or headmistresses to take measurements before granting permission for trousers). Whoever dreamt up skirts knew quite well what he or she was about.

YOU CAN'T BETTER BUTTER

Although I sometimes, when in jovial, waggish and friendly mood, refer to our cultured neighbours across the Channel as 'Frogs', I would like to make it clear that when I write of frogs' legs, I am not indelicately referring to our neighbours' under-pinnings or, if you have French, *jambes*.

It is with nutritional legs that I am dealing and all animal lovers will have rejoiced to see that nowadays in India, before gastronomic use can be made of frogs, they have to be painlessly despatched to the celestial mud-flats by means of a sharp electric shock, as in Death Row, leaving their legs behind them.

As a palatable dish I do not 'go' much on frogs' legs. Long ago in Cannes, aged 22 and eager to sample every varied treat that Life had to offer, including tango teas, I ordered a portion of such legs and found them tasting rather like a fairly dull piece of chicken, part of a spinster Buff Orpington perhaps that, before being called upon to make the supreme sacrifice, had been leading a blameless and sheltered life, keeping herself to herself on a Provençal smallholding.

Now that the entire country seems to think and write and talk of nothing but diets and dieting, I am somewhat surprised never to see frogs' legs on any of the recommended diet sheets that dot our dailies. The calorie content of a couple of legs must be extremely low. Taken with, for lunch, some depressing *nouvelle cuisine* delicacy (half a beetroot smothered in diced carrot), the legs would in no way increase the cholesterol level that agitates so many and one could well become the despair of what one might call the Headquarters of Cholesterol.

I am referring, of course, to the official body called the Butter Council. You raise your eyebrows? So did I mine. You have never heard of the Council? Nor had I until word of their exist-ence reached me via a popular print and I have now become quite fascinated by the thought of them. How many members are there? Where do they meet (Churn House, Tub Lane)? What are they all doing at, say, 10.15 a.m. with a whole buttery day stretching out before them? Many consider the delicious substance to be perilous and so do the official Butter Samplers get paid danger money?

I love to imagine a full Council Meeting, with a Miss Foljamb deftly taking the Minutes: 'The new type of butter pat was agreed to and Mr Bellamy's tasteful impress of a cow couchant was warmly commended. A patented "JIFFO" Electric Butter Spreader ("Watch the butter fly!") was tested and found to be faulty. After Council had moved to another chamber, Major 'Bimbo' Gorringe read an interesting paper on "Lordly Dishes I Have Known". At the end of the meeting, the retiring Chairman, Sir Roderick Globule, was presented with a plated melted butter scoop for, as he amusingly phrased it, "sloshing the stuff onto asparagus"'.

Apart from the enforced dieting that wartime brought with it and which partly lasted, unbelievably now, into 1954, I have never had any time for such nonsense and it is certainly far too late to start now. My tummy has got a splendid tale to tell I can assure you and down the red lane a very fine assortment of foods has gone and will continue to wend its way — fats, fibre, vitamins and protein in the welcome form of steak and kidney pudding (*so* much better than pie: suet, you see), treacle tarts, rich oxtail soups, apple dumplings, great mounds of Devonshire cream: and, as a gracious accompaniment to all these excitements, it's been butter, butter, butter all the way. I wonder if that Council awards medals.

Incidentally, if somebody tells you that something or other 'tastes exactly like butter', just look them straight in the face, inflate your lungs and give a very loud shout of 'BOSH!'. The only thing that tastes like butter is butter. Hence the name.

STAR-CROSSED

I would never, in my modest way, claim ever to have been at the very heart of world events and if I place certain facts before you I do so in no boastful spirit; but all the same at the very moment of my parents' wedding in April, 1906, San Francisco was totally destroyed by a disastrous earthquake and fire, an event which, for my parents, must have added significantly to a week already full, one assumes, of surprises, 'pleasant or unpleasant as the case may be'. Did they, while at the Ilfracombe altar, actually hear distant Richter rumblings? Possibly.

Well then, pray consider the following. Four days before my birth in May, 1910, King Edward VII died, and when I was but a week old, the earth passed, or so I am reliably informed, slap through the tail of Halley's Comet, whizzing aimlessly round for the umpteenth time of asking. There now! Did I, snug in the nursery, positively hear the tinkling pitter-pat of icy particles on the window panes? Maybe. At all events and broadly speaking, when I or a member of my family decides to do something drastic, hold on to your hats.

After all these exceptional excitements, you would think, would you not, that my horoscope and astrological predictions would be lively in the extreme and I myself would be an object of envy. Not at all! The heavenly bodies have in no way singled me out and my weekly forecasts kindly supplied by the press are just as humdrum as anybody else's. 'Wednesday is a good time for taking stock of yourself', it says. The last time I took stock of myself was in 1958 and very depressing it turned out to be. 'On Friday you can afford to spoil yourself a little.' Oh all right.

The remarkable thing about these newspaper star-inspired and behavioural guide-lines is that they can be made to fit neatly into almost any life. 'Make an early start on routine chores' can only refer to my Thursday shopping trip to Newton Abbot.

'You are about to enter on a sociable phase' means morning coffee with the Bultitudes (on patio, if fine) and a generously heaped platter of digestives and custard creams ('Get stuck in, old boy').

I am never too sure about the authoritative technical terms that dot the injunctions. For instance, how jolly or otherwise is 'Mars in Libra is nicely aspected by the New Moon'? It *sounds* all right and a new moon is always pleasing, reminding one as it does of dear Beatrice Lillie warbling away while precariously perched on just such a section of moon, but who can tell? On the other hand, 'Gemini is in Uranus' doesn't sound all right at all and it is wiser not to let the mind wander, but we Taureans know how to hold ourselves in check.

There is, I note, one subject that is totally taboo, in addition to sex, though 'Make a fuss of your partner' is friendly, even with its aura of Mixed Doubles at the club. I refer to food. It's never mentioned. Elsewhere so helpful domestically, with 'Reassess your wardrobe': 'Learn new skills': 'Make life fun': one might live on air for all the stars seem to care. One longs for hints such as 'While Mars is in Taurus, eschew doughnuts and concentrate on bulk protein. With Neptune moving into Pluto, Sunday would be a good day for a dish of crispy-fried parsnips to go with that roast beef'. Nobody now says plain 'fried' except when making a jovial reference to intoxication. It has to be crispy. Nobody will believe me but I recently saw a cook book reference to 'Tree-ripened apples'. Truly. Is this the moment for reminding you of British Rail's 'Dawn-gathered melon'? Yes, it is.

I REMEMBER, I REMEMBER

Vulgar and outspoken persons, engaged in a conversation and wishful to draw attention to a real or imaginary lack of intelligence and understanding in their vis-à-vis, are apt to say, and sometimes they say it with a contemptuous snort, 'You need your head examining'.

There are very few satisfactory ways of rebuffing this piece of impertinence, the words ranking as a sort of Exocet in the conversational armoury. A haughty stare gets you nowhere. You might try 'Look who's talking!' or 'That makes two of us' but they're pretty feeble as counterstrokes. However, if there has been a snort, you might attempt, if you can manage it, a much louder snort back, hanky at the ready.

The phrase 'You need your head examining' should not be confused with 'Oh go and boil your head' which was, in school days long ago, the accepted way of terminating a conversation that had become wearisome to one of the participants. It was sometimes accompanied by a kick or a sharp pinch where one would least expect it. Heigh-ho. One hardly cares to dwell on what boiling heads would mean to a cannibal *chef de cuisine* (adjust your seasonings, dot with lemon wedges and bring to table).

In the surely somewhat limited field of actual head examinings, startling news, long suppressed it would seem, has recently arrived from America to the effect that a portion of Professor Einstein's brain was retained for posterity by a Missouri pathologist and was found to be very abundantly supplied with neurons, which are apparently the cells that do all the thinking and which dreamt up that delightful theory of relativity.

Frankly, I'm not a bit happy about my own neurons. A kind friend did once try to explain the theory to me but my neurons simply weren't up to it and after five seconds I had missed his drift and he had lost me. Perhaps there somewhere exists a helpful booklet, 'Relativity Told to the Kiddies', but meanwhile I've decided to get along as best I can without relativity.

In addition to having my weak neurons exposed for all to scoff at, I should be very sorry to have the rest of my brain examined under a microscope and particularly the section of my head that deals with my memory, cluttered up as it is with piffling facts. Why, for example, should I have remembered for fifty-seven years that that fine actor, Robert Eddison, once told me that in childhood he was invited by a jolly aunt to a matinée of *Rose Marie* and that she sent instructions for the outing on a post-card and in verse, the last lines being 'At half past two the curtain rises, And then you'll see some fine surprises'.

And why should I, who also attended a performance of *Rose Marie*, have remembered, and for over sixty years, that the villainness was a dusky Red Indian called Wanda who sidled sinuously up to the hero, Jim Kenyon, with the seductive words 'You come to Wanda's cabin, maybe?' In the meantime all the strings in the orchestra were scraping that urgently vibrating note that indicates Tension and the whole scene was played behind a gauze curtain to make Wanda seem even more slinky and devilish. You'll want to know whether Mr Kenyon was equal to this assault on his virtue. Luckily I've remembered that too. Yes he was.

There's just so much else in the way of rubbishy recollection. I could tell you the names of school friends who actually owned steam locomotives for their model railways rather than humdrum clockwork ones. If really pushed I could provide my grandmother's registration number at the Army & Navy Stores. If requested (and you'd be mad to), I could recite a long poem from the 1920 omnibus edition of *Chums* about a highwayman and which began ' 'Twas Christmas Eve at the Anchor Inn, Guests were many and loud the din'. I could relate full details of a disastrous 1919 tea-party when a hugely greedy lady called Mrs Ham was seen to be putting strawberry jam on her cucumber sandwich and, wishing to display my scintillating wit, I said 'He feedeth the hungry with good things'. This was considered to be sacrilegious and I was dismissed from the table.

But what happened yesterday is already a blur. And as for a week ago . . . ! Indeed, what has been happening in the last twelve months is already dim and mysterious. Just as well, I dare say.

I said 'He feedeth the hungry with good things'

ABSENT FRIENDS

Although it is now some years since the BBC wireless authorities decided to sweep her so ruthlessly away, I still feel — and it
was at tea-time that she first came to us, kindly repeating herself
next morning — an emptiness, a void, a yearning hunger for
the vocal doings of dear Mrs Dale of Parkwood Hill; Mary
Dale, wife of Dr Jim.

In their blindness the BBC never rated this wholesome and
quite exemplary woman as highly as *The Archers* and she was
denied (the insult still rankles) a Sunday Omnibus but her diary
entries ('Sally called and over brunch we discussed new
cretonne patterns for Virginia Lodge') went perfectly with
scones, strawberry jam and a coffee sponge, items that themselves figured so freely ('Mrs Mountford gobbled up half our
cake') in the social whirl of what must have been, I think, the
Chingford area, though some experts have placed the Dales at
Chadwell Heath.

Then, after one had barely recovered from the shock of a
bleak and Daleless world, there came another body blow — the
departure of Meg Mortimer, the linchpin, nay the very rock
upon which the Crossroads Motel itself was built. But how was
she to go? There were alarming rumours of ATV employees
being seen at dead of night digging property graves in deserted
churchyards and a violent death was forecast for her (many
feared an incineration in the Motel bonfire) but in the end she
just left, waving violently, for Australia in the *QE II*, only just
missing being diverted to the Falklands.

And now, bless me, if we aren't going to have to face another
tragic absentee from our TV screens in the sturdy person of Len
Fairclough, the efficient and delightful jobbing builder of
Coronation Street, husband of Rita and owner of the news-
agent's where shy Mavis so twitteringly presides. It is said that
he is to be 'killed off', though that may be just a figure of

speech or, if you have French, a *façon de parler* and he may be allowed to drift off to another district and jobbing build elsewhere.

But stay! I have an idea and really rather an intriguing one. Why should we so sadly have to lose sight of these fascinating characters in whom and on whom so many of us have lavished such an interest and affection? They live for us still and so why cannot they be allowed to pop up somewhere else? Len is quite a jack of all trades and he would be an invaluable and genial presence on the bridge of the BBC's *Triangle* ship, hitherto manned by a crew of grumpy crosspatches and where absolutely everything keeps going wrong (how they ever get to sea at all is quite a puzzle and personally I'm going by air).

Another idea! Why can't there be a kind of cross-breeding between one series and another, a stimulating intermingling of established characters (I would give a lot to be able to read one of Mrs Dale's letters home after spending a typical week in the *Dynasty* household). Hilda Ogden, much done up and with not a curler on view, would make an arresting figure behind the Crossroads Reception Desk, wildly inquisitive about every resident and deeply impressed by the motel's distinctive mauve décor and luxurious 'fittings'.

I am far from sure how well Sue Ellen, even in one of her better weeks, would go down in Parkwood Hill ('We've got a Mrs J. R. Ewing staying. She's . . . well . . . a little *different*'). A medium Cyprus sherry was the preferred drink at Virginia Lodge, and not very much of it at that, and sherry isn't really a lot of use to an inside accustomed to nine strongish dry martinis before lunch. One episode might end with Sue Ellen pinching from Jim's surgery a bottle of surgical alcohol and making a pass at the deaf gardener, Monument, before falling flat on her face in the begonias.

Concerning the right niche for Sue Ellen's husband, the dreaded J.R., there is no sort of doubt. Much of the vigorous life, emotional and plain, in *Crossroads* swirls round the motel garage (not many cars ever on show but I dare say we catch them at slack periods) and here J.R., with his flair and knowledge of the oil business, would be in his element. No doubt he could speedily strike up what I suppose we must call 'a working relationship' with the manageress, Sharon, herself no slouch when Dan Cupid calls.

Why not treat it as a fireside game and get going on your own? Mix them all up — Benny, Miss Ellie, Ray, Bo'sun (the Dale dog), Mr Hunter, Sid, Lucy and Diane's dreadful brother.

INDOOR GAMES

Among the multitude of Life's accepted pleasures that have never come my way (hang-gliding, fatherhood, scaling the Matterhorn), the playing of Bingo must, as a deprivation, rank pretty high. I rather doubt whether I would now be able to master the rules of this treat. In childhood it took me quite some time to learn the intricacies of Snap and, bemused by the glossy magnificence of the playing cards, I was a plucky loser of game after game.

At Bingo I gather that at some, no doubt critical, point somebody calls out 'Legs eleven' but then to an old and seasoned cricketer such as myself, this merely sounds like something from a fixture list (June 23rd: The School v Major Legge's XI).

Film fans have now become regretfully accustomed to having many of their provincial Astorias, Odeons and Rexes ('Reges' for Classicists) turned into Bingo establishments, jammed to the doors with players whose quiet and dedicated devotion, eyes down as if in prayer, to the matter in hand entitles them to be regarded as 'congregations' and will remind ecclesiastical historians, sadly perhaps, of the fervent church-going and packed edifices of the last century.

Struggling as I do to keep abreast of all that is finest and noblest in our modern civilisation, I see that Bingo has now spread its wings and can be played, with the aid of various popular daily newspapers, by post and telephone. A quick scanning of the instructions (Have You Sent for Your Master Bingo Booklet?) and the exciting lures (You Can Be World Champion!) convinces me that the whole profitable enterprise is quite beyond me, a social outcast yet again.

So, in my case and in clement weather, it is back to the dear old croquet lawn, coloured balls whizzing blithely to and fro and the only athletic game where champions can well be elderly and 'pegging out' just means winning.

However, in the rainy season (September to April), I am thinking of giving, as an alternative to Bingo, some of the Indoor Games Parties that were so frequent in my youth. They began at 3 p.m. (Tea, 4.30) and for these hostesses insisted on pairing everybody off. Handed on your arrival a label with ADAM on it, you hunted about for the girl labelled EVE ('I'm Joan Lightbody. Who are you?'). ROMEO sought out JULIET ('Oh, hooray, Enid, it's you!'). One's extensive knowledge of history came in useful here and nobody announcing himself as being NELSON would ever have dreamt of looking about for poor old Lady Nelson.

Clutching a scoring card and firmly dragooned and directed by a hostess shrieking 'Now, all of you go and guess the smells in the morning-room' you moved off and found yourself facing, strung on a line across the room, a series of small opaque bags which were being eagerly and unhygienically sniffed at by fellow competitors. Feeling the bags was not permitted and cheating was frowned on ('But I didn't touch it, truly, Mrs Bumstead'). The smells were usually established fragrances such as coffee and mint and lavender but sometimes there was a ha-ha-ha one (pepper).

The fun was fast and furious. From a distance of twelve feet you tried to throw playing cards into a top hat. You sucked up peas through a straw and deposited them, with a time-limit, in a saucer. You played that memory test, Kim's Game, with treasured Bumstead knick-knacks set out on a tray. you unravelled anagrams rather unfortunately referred to as JUMBLED PARTS — ENOS, BELOW, INCH, HOT TAR, CAKE PEN. It will be clear to ace crossword-solvers that BELOW is capable of two solutions, but ELBOW was the wise one to put down.

As the afternoon wore on, and I use the verb deliberately, it was 'Tea, everybody', and as the gingersnaps and flapjacks went down the red lanes, darkness fell, often bringing with it Colonel Bumstead ('Oh good, here's Ambrose'), a crimson-faced 'Something in the City' and who, determined to be kind and jolly, led a rumbustical game of Murder or Sardines, a pastime so graphically and memorably described by our revered Poet Laureate.

On second thoughts, however, perhaps I'll give Bingo a try.

ANY OLD IRON?

Autumn may indeed be the season of mists and mellow fruitfulness but it is also, for reasons provided by itself, the season of jumble sales. A sharp autumnal increase in rainfall and general dampness alerts everybody, by means of drips on the head, to the porous state of the church roof, or the village hut roof, or both, and the defiant financial answer to these pressing repair requirements is almost always a jumble sale.

A roneoed notice pushed through the letter-box, with 'Will call Tuesday a.m.' hastily scribbled on it, excitingly prepares one for the forthcoming and communal festivity and gives one time to rout out whatever jumble wasn't routed out last time and hand it to the collector on Tuesday a.m. Jumble sales are blessedly anonymous. Nobody bothers about which tattered article belonged to whom. That broken tie-rack or chipped mug or size 15 shirt ('It seems to have shrunk') won't be traced back.

The saleable items, laid out on trestle tables in the Vicarage garden do not exactly lift the heart. The most depressing object I have seen was, quite simply, a tooth-brush, an old toothbrush, pink-handled and with flattened bristles. Whoever, no matter how hard-pressed dentally, would want a brush that had known healthful activity around another's molars? I do remember that during the war, and for cleaning intimate parts of Sam Browne belts and webbing equipment, an old toothbrush was sometimes handy, but we are not at war now, much though it may sometimes seem like it.

As everybody knows who has ever run a jumble sale, the really essential thing is to prevent the vicar's macintosh from getting accidentally sold as jumble. The good man comes hurrying in, having snatched a precious moment or two between a christening and a Churching of Women and, before going the rounds of the stalls, quickly lays his macintosh down by mistake on a table marked EVERYTHING HERE 10p. By the time duty calls again (confirmation address in the church hall and next Sunday's sermon, 'Let your light shine', to prepare), the macintosh has been snapped up.

Sometimes a jumble sale gets ideas above its station and sprouts, in addition to jumble, 'produce' stalls and cake stalls and jams and cuttings and pots of house plants, and when this happens, everybody feels that the sale is sufficiently impressive for it to be 'opened' by somebody.

I sometimes wonder where unsold articles go until they make a reappearance at the next jumble sale. I have now seen, three years running, a jumbo elephant table-lamp (it holds a naked bulb aloft in its trunk) that, though nice enough in its way, nobody has yet been able to find house-room for. Where does it go? Is there some oubliette, or corner of the church crypt, or a disused tomb where the unwanted remain, like forgotten stars whose day is over, until they burst forth once more into the limelight?

I myself make a bee line for the large pile of gramophone records, all ancient 78s, that always shows up, with different ones every year. If you're lucky, endless treasures are to be found — Peter Dawson rumbling away about Drake Going West, a tasteful trio scraping out Gems from Gounod (in music-halls you could always tell if a trio was going to be tasteful — it had draped curtains and a standard lamp), one of those hilariously unfunny 'laughing' records, or the vibrant chest notes of Dame Clara Butt rattling the grooves with 'Land of Hope and Glory'.

MEALS AWHEEL

The news that British Rail, thrashing about in what some pessimists see as its death agonies, has had the cheek to raise its buffet car prices yet again and now charges 26p (5s 2d in proper money and did you ever hear of such a thing!) for a small plastic beakerette of coffee, complete with sugar capsuline, spillable milk cartonette and disposable spoon, has set reformers feverishly thinking of possible train refreshment alternatives.

One of them, and excellent it is too, is to farm out the catering facilities to persons other than B.R. and I see it suggested that 'small family concerns' should take over this or that train. Well, although only a family of one, I am perfectly ready to help and my journalistic calling takes me at regular intervals to London on the 3.56 train from Exeter, just the ideal moment for tea.

For some time now, my tomato sandwiches (a mistake to get them too damp) and my home-made Honey Clusters (basically Rice Crispies, disguised) have been quite a talking point among my appreciative social circle in Devon and I am fully prepared to make large batches of both and dispense them as required, and for a very modest sum, with the happy faces my true reward.

Perhaps I could join up with other families for the return journey (11.35 a.m.) from Paddington and we could have a duty roster, with the train's Menu of the Day (crab vol-au-vent, braised shoulder, meat balls Norwegian style) chalked up on one of those blackboards which B.R. normally reserve for informing us of inconveniences (29 trains cancelled, and a mini-derailment at Crewe). Though sandwiches are really my forte, I could, if pushed, manage turkey croquettes, and from time to time I construct a sort of cheese omelette but am far too conscientious to expose the latter to public view and actually charge money for it.

If given the chance, who can doubt that large firms, accustomed to giving satisfaction and to making money, would make a splendid job of the catering, with the grander trains named after them — the Fortnum Flyer to Bournemouth (sirloin steak and Kipper Scramble as a savoury), the Sainsbury Special to Cheltenham (grain-fed poultry in every delicious form) and the Marks Meteor to Durham (a very fine range of cellophane-hugged Convenience Foods). Some trains could, by their very names, reveal the culinary availabilities on board, with the Lancashire Hot-Pot to Bolton, and a wild rush for the Devilled Trotters to Skegness.

But this is only playing with the subject for we all know perfectly well that by far the best thing would be simply to hand over all B.R. restaurants and buffets to the Women's Institutes. No rubbishy beakerettes here but enormous china mugs and large brown teapots and warm, encouraging voices saying 'Let me top you up, dear'. Payment might be, as sometimes at church fêtes, by negotiation: 'Now let's see, you had tea, three of my raisin crunchies, and one of Mrs Harper's flapjacks. Would 35p be too much?'

For the more solid and main course W.I. dishes, there could be exciting announcements (and just picture the dribbles!) over the loudspeaker, keeping everybody abreast with current progress in the swaying *cuisine*: 'You'll all be glad to know, ladies and gentlemen, that Mrs Henderson's Yorkshire is rising admirably, while Mrs Dunderdale is just about to float her suet dumplings onto the gently bubbling surface of her boiled silverside. Meanwhile, Mrs Purkiss will be circulating among you with her tray of attractive Starters. Why not try a *bouchée* of tuna mousse, or I can warmly recommend her stuffed eggs'.

Although some people advocate introducing commerce into rail travel and suggest that firms sell their products awheel, I rather doubt myself whether, as one flies through Castle Cary at 90 m.p.h., it is the absolutely ideal moment for purchasing a pocket calculator or a matching set of golf clubs.

But I do have a novel and cheerful suggestion of my own to place before you, inspired by the homely and somewhat old-fashioned (and all the better for it) world of the W.I.

Briefly, it is this. Why not a *thé dansant* in the guard's van? I could easily bring along my dear old portable (we'd all take it in turns to crank the thing up) and a nostalgic selection of 78s — 'The Bam Bam Bammy Shore', 'Hesitation Waltz', 'The Tickle Toe' and 'I Love my Chilli-Bom-Bom'. I'll join you there just as soon as the last of my sandwiches has been sold. Save me the tango.

Why not a *thé dansant* in the guard's van?

I'M IN CHARGE

Many and varied are the chores that fall to one as one progresses timidly along Life's boulder-strewn pathway and it may come as an astonishment to some to learn that I, boastful as it may be of me to make the claim, have in the past done my stint as a cricket umpire.

It was during my happy days as an Oundle schoolmaster when, very occasionally and when they couldn't find anybody else, I was asked to don that impressive white coat and take my stand at the popping crease (I think: anyway, that white line).

The matches involved were junior house matches, needle contests with no quarter given, and now, with the cricketing season at its thrilling peak, I am happy to pass on, in my friendly way, some useful umpiring tips.

The essential thing, and right from the start, is to impress your personality on the game and it was therefore my custom to adjudge the very first ball of the match to be, and very loudly, a 'NO BALL!' I warmly recommend this practice. It gives confidence where no confidence actually is. If you care to add, to the disgruntled bowler as he walks back, 'Watch that left leg of yours!', well and good. Perhaps, '*Do* watch that left leg!' would give a greater sense of urgency, but that's up to you.

Incidentally, I have never yet been able to get anybody to tell me authoritatively whether a ball can be at one and the same time a 'No ball' and a 'Wide', and so I usually signalled both to the scorer. All this keeps bowlers on their toes and arouses in the spectators a stimulating air of expectancy. I have known housemasters almost fall off their shooting-sticks with what I took to be pleasurable excitement.

The next essential is to allow the very first appeal. It may be LBW, caught, run out or 'hit wicket' (far too seldom done: *such* a merry clattering sound!). What are batsmen for if not to be given out and so, when the fielders all start shouting 'How's that?' or 'How was it?' or bark out some such interrogative, answer clearly and immediately, 'OUT!' Umpires normally just raise a finger and I don't think they're supposed to speak, but I always did. Sometimes, if doubt seemed to exist, I said, 'Obviously out. Kindly leave the pitch', adding, if in the mood, 'Hard cheese'. This too keeps everybody on the qui vive and keenly awaiting the next surprise dismissal.

In my own young day, and I speak of the 1920s when nobody would have dreamt of rubbing the ball ('How dare you tamper with school property!'), let alone spit on it, those waiting their turn, brief though it might be, at the wicket and were not required to work the scoring apparatus (mysteriously called the Tallywag), used to play a game called French cricket. It merely involved protecting the legs with a bat while somebody shied a ball at your ankles and it could be played by as few as two persons, a sadly feeble version of our national game and invented in an off moment by our sometimes rather misguided neighbours.

Now that we are all in the Common Market together, can we not encourage the French to take up, or *épouser*, this healthful summer pursuit? I do rather wonder what French terms would seem the right cricketing ones. *'Qu'est-ce que c'est que ça?'* hasn't somehow got quite the right ring for 'How's that?' The French, a very critical race, have never been slow to apportion guilt and so possibly *'Coupable? Oui ou non?'* would fill the bill.

The actual field positions present no sort of difficulty — *première glissade* (first slip), *jambe énorme* (long leg), *lunatique milieu sur* (silly mid-on) and our saucy Continental friends would certainly see extra cover-point as *cache-sexe additionnelle*.

One poser remains — what to do about the word 'Stumps' with its hint of some disaster involving truncated limbs. As all keen cricketers will know, 'What time are stumps?' means, and oh what a blessed moment it was for the less keen, 'At what hour does the game end?'

Would *'A Quelle heure sont les membres mutilés?'* mean very much in, say, Toulouse? Time will tell *(Temps racontera)*.

IN VINO VERITAS

Those of us who have been anxiously worrying that the nation's resolute character, sapped by entry into the Common Market, may not be quite what it was will have received a further jolt from the announcement that wine, that effeminate drink so well suited to our nearest neighbours across the channel, is now being increasingly consumed by all classes in our fair land.

Can it really be true that beer, the good, solid, nourishing beverage that is so typical of us, is on the way out? Are we going to have to get accustomed in pubs to hearing, as a burly worker fresh off the shift approaches the bar and the ceremonial words have been said by the proprietor, 'What's it to be, Fred?', the shaming reply, 'I'd like a small glass of that amusing little Barsac of yours, George'.

When Frankie Howerd appeared as Charley's Aunt, he spoke what must have been, I fancy, an invented line of his own and when old Mr Spettigue said courteously to him, 'Would you care to join me in a glass of wine, Madam?', he replied, 'Yes, if there's room'. This seems to me to be a splendidly frivolous attitude to the whole subject of wine, a subject taken so seriously by so many.

There are all those wine adjectives to start off with — sturdy, well-balanced, cheeky, provoking, fruity, lots to say for itself, finely rounded, plenty of backbone, full-bodied — adjectives which could equally well and more profitably be applied to the members of the Welsh Rugger XV.

I had to start drinking the stuff at a relatively early age. When holidaying in France, everybody was urged to drink the *vin ordinaire* as the *eau ordinaire* was said to be tainted. Everybody knew some terrifying tale of somebody else's Aunt Jessie or Uncle Neddy who had recklessly drunk water from the tap in their Paris hotel bedroom, had come out instantly in a crimson rash, swollen up like a balloon and gone pop.

You couldn't be too careful and for confirmed water-lovers it was always down the hatch with Evian and Vichy and Perrier, even though rascally frog waiters, ever out to make an extra *sou* or two, were known to fill the empty bottles from the nearest stream.

I like wine but there are all sorts of things connected with its drinking that I am not a bit keen on. When, at dinner, I see somebody raise a glass of wine to his nose, wave it to and fro beneath his distended nostrils and then start sniffing and snuffling at it like the Hound of the Baskervilles, it is all I can do not to retaliate by raising my plate in the same manner and sniff and snuffle at my brussels sprouts.

Then there comes the first taste of wine, the glazed look of concentration and the distasteful rolling round the tongue as though it were a mouthwash. No brussels sprout could stand up to that sort of thing, or would wish to. Then there are the gulping and the lip-smacking and the pompous vinous pronouncements: 'I always say that you just can't go wrong with a really earthy Beaujolais, it has such poise and strikes a balance between savour and flavour and bouquet'.

There is only one opinion that I would put forward in connection with wine and it was well illustrated at a dinner that I was invited to attend in London. It was some learned society function or other and, in the middle of the main course, the claret ran out. Our chairman, a great wine expert, rose graciously to his feet and said something like, 'Gentlemen, a choice awaits us. We can now either go on to the 1962 Clos de Cloaque or the 1963 Château Poubelle. There is, on the other hand, the 1964 Nuit St Vitus, or the . . .' I could see my neighbour shifting angrily in his chair and suddenly he jumped up. 'Stop all that ruddy rubbish', he shouted, 'and just give us what there's *most* of.' My very own feelings, and crisply expressed.

MIXED MUNCHABLES

One likes, in one's outgoing and unselfish way, to take a friendly interest in the social doings of others and for many years now I have been following closely the instances of lavish government hospitality (at some periods, it's been just beano after beano) as reported to us in the public prints. It is, after all, hospitality paid for by kind old you and me and I like to make sure that our cash is being laid out in a sensible manner.

Indeed, I was so struck once by a biggish dinner party thrown during Mr Heath's memorable regime at No. 10 that I wrote a polite letter asking him about the purpose of the gathering, together with details of the menu, the wines and floral decorations, if any, but my letter must have miscarried for answer came there none. Or perhaps they were all too busy tidying up and wondering what to do with the left-overs.

On that occasion, the rosy looks of the chubbychops host led one to think that there was no stint in the calorie-packed goodies. As to the undivulged menu, I seem to see a nourishing and *croûton*-dotted soup (oxtail, possibly, or maybe a cream of vegetable), a good firm fish such as halibut with a buttery prawn sauce, and then a lordly baron of beef with all the trimmings ('Come, Foreign Secretary, another dollop of Yorkshire?') And as to a pudding, what else could it be but cabinet? Three different wines, would you think? But one so longs for the actual facts.

I am thinking of writing again to No. 10 for September saw a quite unbridled outburst of governmental party-giving and among the merry festivities was a luncheon for Japan's Foreign Minister. We know from the proliferating Chinese take-aways what the Chinese eat, but the Japanese stomach presents an enigma and so one flies, naturally, to the opera *Madam Butterfly* for information. The heroine, Cio-Cio-San, certainly employs a male cook, though the music and action do not permit him to mention menus. Lieutenant B. F. Pinkerton, fresh from an American battleship and plainly full of beefburgers, gives us a soulful aria which goes 'Amore o grillo', but the grillo part can hardly refer, I think, to any foodstuffs actually grilled on stage. Therefore doubt, alas, remains.

Also to be found at our country's groaning board have been the Cameroon Ambassador, an Italian Minister (tinned ravioli were last week On Offer in our Devon store and so I could have helped here), the Ambassador of Uruguay — peppery sauces would have been the gracious thing — and assorted happy munchers from the U.S.A., Sweden (made to feel at home, I trust, with mashed swedes), Portugal, Hong Kong, Oman, St Lucia and Greece.

Our leader herself has been no slouch and earlier on she gave a largely French lunch. How good is Mrs Thatcher's grasp of the language? One imagines a reputable O Level in a firmly English accent, perhaps helped out with the sort of thing that used to go on at a girls' school French-speaking table watched over by Mademoiselle: 'Passez-moi les spuds' and 'Après vous avec les condiments'.

And the menu? One so hopes that it was something really tasty — perhaps crab vol-au-vent, a roast saddle, and then baked Alaska with strawbugs. After all, the French, whatever else they may or may not have done, did more or less invent food.

Which of us would not have wished to be present at one of the festivities in Scotland. The Minister for Health and Social Work was host at an evening reception 'on the occasion of the meeting of the Alcohol Education and Research Council'. However does one get oneself elected to this jolly body? I am perfectly ready to submit myself for further education in such matters as gin slings, John Collins, Scotch on the rocks and Bloody Marys. And selfless as ever, I am quite prepared to be very fully researched into.

WELCOME BACK

It is cheering news indeed that the BBC is going, at the urgent request of probably the older type of listener, to bring back *Music While You Work*, that joyous half-hour cascade of popular melody and the indestructible tunes of yesteryear and one's anticipatory boots are already tapping to the insistent rhythms.

Introduced to the public at that grim and backs-to-the-wall time of June, 1940, it seems likely that each individual musical number was chosen as a special incentive to some particular group of workers: 'Pennies from Heaven' (the Mint): 'I'll See You Again' (ophthalmic technicians): 'I've Got You Under my Skin' (hypodermic needle makers), and it is possible that the music-hall's 'Every little movement has a message of its own' was aimed at toilers in the field of sewage and sanitation.

One does so hope that this welcome revival of an old favourite is merely the beginning of a string of jolly resuscitations and that before long the good Mrs Dale and her Diary will be back with us. The series might begin again with Mrs Freeman (Mrs Dale's sprightly old mother, you recall) getting a Greetings Tele-message from the Queen on her 105th birthday and at a great Parkwood Hill gathering of the Dales, all purple in the face with Cyprus sherry and munching away, as of yore, at the remains of the meat-loaf while beyond the patio, the gardener, Monument, now 98, wheezes his resentful way through the calceolarias.

And, in the world of television, our grateful thanks must go to Channel 4 for reintroducing us, willy-nilly though the action may have been, to the restful Interlude. Do you remember long ago those pleasing and between-items BBC shots of a potter's wheel in motion, a windmill gently turning, water quietly flowing in a stretch of the Thames generously stocked with swans, and the sea lazily lapping the beaches of, at a guess, Margate?

Channel 4, momentarily devoid of advertisements, confined itself to what at first sight looked like a colourful display of wine-gums but turned out on closer inspection to be fractured and kaleidoscopic portions of the title 'Channel 4', distributed higgledy-piggledy as in a jig-saw. Or the ensemble could have been taken for a modern abstract painting called, maybe, 'Mood: 1979'.

No matter. The thing was that it didn't budge about and it acted on viewers, so constantly dazzled elsewhere with violent movement, like a soothing eye-bath, while the music that accompanied it was entirely appropriate to the happy and somnolent and all too short moments of peace. Is it too much to hope that the dreaded cable television will have at least one channel on which nothing at all happens? Just country shots of cows and sheep going calmly about their business to the lilting strains of Eric Coates and with just the occasional bleat or moo thrown in.

What else in the wireless would one welcome back? In pre-war days the distinguished cellist, Beatrice Harrison, used nobly to lug her instrument deep into the Surrey woods. There she scraped and plucked away with the intention of encouraging those nightingales who had not instantly fled, put off by the the sounds of bodies crashing through the undergrowth, to give vocally of their best. It was always alleged that some listeners mistook the liquid notes for what was then a permanent hazard called 'interference' and hastily switched stations, but as a museum piece it would be fun to hear it all again, if another intrepid cellist can be found, not to speak of nightingales.

What, I wonder, would people now make of the superb Gillie Potter, the Sage of Hogs Norton and a treasured memory? What of 'A. J. Alan', the mysterious civil servant who invented the comical radio story and always insisted that a lighted candle be put in the studio in case all the lights fused? How very agreeable to find that, recently revived, *Round the Horne* has seemed even more hilarious than before, which is indeed saying something. There is still a great deal to be said for non-visual humour, as a few comedians, relentlessly exposed on the box, are beginning to discover.